PREVIOUS BOOKS BY NICOLE A. TAYLOR

The Last O.G. Cookbook

The Up South Cookbook

WATER MELON & RED BIRDS

A COOKBOOK FOR JUNETEENTH AND BLACK CELEBRATIONS

NICOLE A. TAYLOR

SIMON & SCHUSTER

NEW YORK LONDON TORONTO SYDNEY NEW DELHI

Simon & Schuster
1230 Avenue of the Americas
New York, NY 10020

Photography by Beatriz da Costa
Food Styling by Victoria Granoff
Prop Styling by Gerri Williams
Poem p.xiv by Omar Tate
Photograph p.107 by Alexa Rivera
Author Photograph by Adrian Franks

First Simon & Schuster hardcover edition May 2022

SIMON & SCHUSTER and colophon are registered trademarks of Simon &
Schuster, Inc.

For information about special discounts for bulk purchases,
please contact Simon & Schuster Special Sales at 1-866-506-1949 or
business@simonandschuster.com.

The Simon & Schuster Speakers Bureau can bring authors to your live
event. For more information or to book an event, contact the Simon &
Schuster Speakers Bureau at 1-866-248-3049 or visit our website at
www.simonspeakers.com.

Design by George McCalman and Aliena Cameron of McCalmanCo

Manufactured in the United States of America

10 9 8 7 6 5 4 3 2 1

Library of Congress Cataloging-in-Publication Data has been applied for.

ISBN 978-1-9821-7621-1
ISBN 978-1-9821-7622-8 (ebook)

ACKNOWLEDGMENTS

The road to get the recipes on the page, to get real stories and historical moments in this cookbook, has been a zigzagged line. I spent a lot of time away from my young son trying to make sense of a niche holiday that is now a national holiday. I tripled back on recipe testing to make sure I got things right. The weight of the world around me almost broke my spirit as I produced a photo shoot, managed budgets, and interacted with recipe developers and recipe testers; many times during this process, I gave in to self-doubt, and I lost the very joy I write about over and over. Then a red bird would appear—my ancestors would sing to me and strut around my backyard, reminding me to rest and then try again. Thank you, ancestors.

The secret sauce to everything I do is the encouragement and positivity of my brilliant partner in life, Adrian. He is the person I run to to make everything better. God has been good to me, and my prince, Garvey Crown, is my proof.

Many dear friends and colleagues have carried me through this journey, and completing this cookbook is their victory, too: Gabrielle Fulton Ponder, Reginald Dye, Stacey West, Lesley Ware, Jordan A. Colbert, Brooklyn Zoo Group Text, J. J. Johnson, Yahdon Israel, Adriana Velez, Charlotte Druckman, Shyretha and Mike Sheats, Scott Barton, Porsche Williams, Kristina Gill, Bryant Terry, Osayi Endolyn, Cynthia Greenlee, Von Diaz, Keia Mastrianni, Michael Twitty, Toni Tipton-Martin, Gabrielle

E. W. Carter, Roz Bentley, Therese Nelson, Aki Baker, and Melissa Danielle. Plus my therapist, who for twenty months listened to the highs and lows of my professional and personal journey toward wholeness.

I reminded myself a hundred times that the magnetic energy of this cookbook began with Dawn Davis while she was a VP at Simon & Schuster and founder of 37 INK. Thank you to Dana Canedy and Emily Graff at S&S for keeping me on track. Plus, much gratitude to LaSharah Bunting for impactful comments.

I was fortunate enough to work with a crew of top-notch creatives in the business to bring this cookbook to life: Jenn de la Vega (patient recipe developer), Lolis E. Elie (manuscript doctor, editor, and eleventh-hour savior), Laura Arnold (recipe editor), Gerri Williams (prop stylist and a cool breeze on a spring day), Victoria Granoff (one of the best to do it!), Beatriz da Costa (the one photographer who gave me the old friend vibe), and Ali (right hand to George, I'll miss our weekly meetings). Thank you, George—your artistry helped me push the boundaries of what a Black cookbook can be.

Believe it or not, I never thought this cookbook concept was viable, but my longtime literary agent, Sharon Bowers, kept circling back to this idea, and I finally gave in. I remember her saying, "A Juneteenth cookbook will be your magnum opus." We shall see.

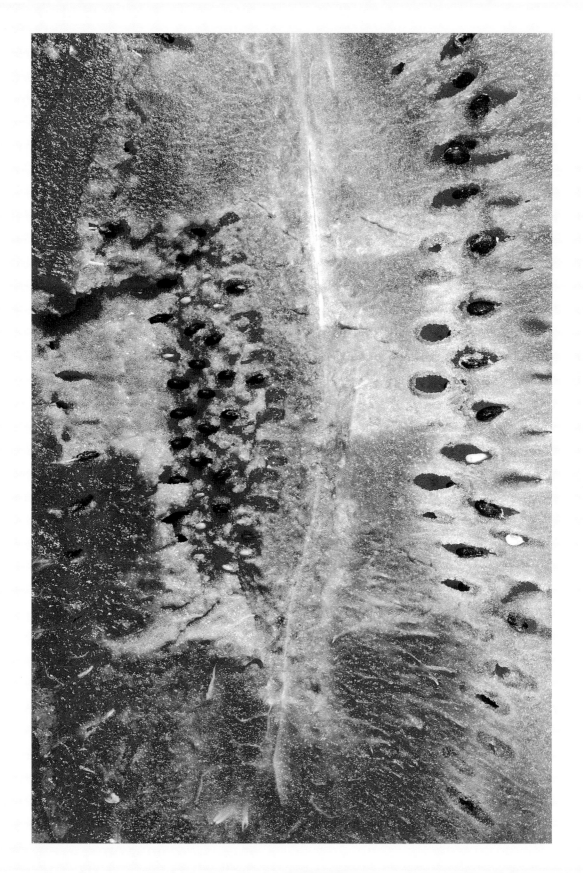

CONTENTS

FOREWORD

PART 1
INTRODUCTION

PART 2
JUNETEENTH GADGETS & PANTRY

RECIPE LIST

Spice Blends, Hot Sauces & Pickled Things

All-Purpose Seasoning
Lemon Pepper Seasoning
Sweet Potato Seasoning
Chili Powder
Chicken Salt
Citrus Verbena Salt
Peppercorn Rub
Dukkah
Fish Fry Mix
Fig Vinegar BBQ Sauce
Rhubarb BBQ Sauce
Peach & Molasses Sauce
Romesco
NAT's Red Hot Sauce
Salsa Verde
Harissa
Green Garlic Chimichurri
Quick-Pickles
    Blueberries
    Squash Spears
    Banana Peppers
    Purple Carrots
    Red Onions

Red Drinks

Ginger Beer
Watermelon Ginger Beer
Marigold Gin Sour
Strawberry Lemonade
Afro Egg Cream
    Hibiscus Tea

Maroon Margarita
Sweet Potato Spritz
Blueberry & Bay Leaf Tonic
    Lemon Cordial
Miso Bloody Mary

Festivals & Fairs

Funnel Cake with Apple Topping
Corn Dogs
Zucchini Corn Dogs
Turnip Corn Balls
Tornado Sweet Potatoes
Beer-Battered Shrimp
Savory Elephant Ears
Chorizo–Corn Chip Nachos
Wavy Fries with Blue Cheese Dip & Lemon Pepper
Rodeo Turkey Legs

Cookout & BBQ

Meatless Baked Beans
Pork Chops with Dukkah
Caraway Butter Trout
Peach & Molasses Chicken
Peppercorn Rib Eye
Grilled Oysters
Late-Night Steak Tostada
Very Green Coleslaw with Grilled Peppers
Apricot Lamb Chops with Green Garlic Chimichurri
Beef Ribs with Harissa
Watermelon Kebabs with Citrus Verbena Salt

Victory Chicken Burgers
Fancy Mushrooms
Pork Ribs with a BBQ Sauce Flight

Potato, Green & Fruit Salads

Plum & Super Greens Pesto Salad
Southern-ish Potato Salad
New Age Wedge
Carrots & Mustard Flowers
Summer Peas, Green Beans & Corn Salad
Crab & Egg Salad
Tomato & Eggplant Salad
Cantaloupe & Feta

Snow Cones, Ice Pops & Ice Cream

Cucumber Granita
Snow Cones
    Hibiscus Sichuan
    Marigold
    Purple Sweet Potato
Liberation Sundae
    Dairy-Free Chocolate Sorbet
    Rhubarb Compote
Raspberry Yogurt Pops
Roasted Nectarine Sundae
    Honey Vanilla Ice Cream
    Pistachio Brittle
    Caramel Sauce
Corn Ice Cream Sandwiches

Cake! Cake! Cake! (And a Couple of Pies)

Peach Crumble Pie Bars
Peach Crumb Cake
Strawberry Hand Pies
Strawberry & Black Pepper Slab Pie
Strawberry Sumac Cake
Radish & Ginger Pound Cake
Florida Punch Bowl Cake
Kaylah's Tea Cakes
Moscato Pound Cake
Blueberry & Beef Puff Pies
Devil's Food Icebox Cake
Blackberry Eton Mess
Chile Marshmallow Pies
Peanut Butter Spiced Whoopie Pies

Everyday Juneteenth

Coffee Daiquiri
Fruits of Juneteenth Smoothie Bowl
Pecan Waffles
Yellow Squash & Cheddar Biscuits
Pretzel Fried Chicken
Broiler Salmon with Romesco
Garlicky Okra & Rice
Sour Cream & Chive Cornbread
Cherries Jubilee

FOREWORD

My friend Nicole Taylor has a curiosity that is infectious and tenacious, and matched only by her love for her people. For Us. This particular combination has been to the great benefit of the US food writing canon, to the professional food writing community, and to YOU.

The upside is clear: we're getting a perspective that doesn't just place us—it grounds us. I'm always asking myself, *Is this the right narrator for this story?* With Nicole, the answer is always yes, because I know that those stories are embodied. We know who it's for, and we know she's invested.

These recipes are illustrative of her gifts, moving us seamlessly from the historic to the contemporary, with ingredients and rhetoric together reinforcing a clear thesis—"I put on for my people." In this book, a story of place is articulated in the composition of each recipe, from the dishes to the spritzes. And as someone who considers her a beloved dining companion, it is a pleasure to read these very smart recipes, which are full of surprising and delightful ingredient combinations, organized in sections curated with the rigor of a MOMA exhibit.

In *Watermelon & Red Birds: A Cookbook for Juneteenth and Black Celebrations*, we are bound to celebration. We know well the hardship story, and are ready to write a different story. What you're reading—this book—is just that. I hope you will take the opportunity, as I am, to celebrate Nicole, as an author, a friend, and a north star on heart-centered work.

—Stephen Satterfield, founder of Whetstone Media, host of
   High on the Hog

HOT LINKS & RED DRINKS

My people came to this country linked
Forming bonds where there were none
Previously, untwined forever bound
Now to one another, swaying down
Below in the belly of a foreign beast
Channeling through the big pond
My people were hot, sweaty, and sick
Lined, bound eternally by the worst
That God had given to man
Their blood spilled into the ocean
Swirling with the tides
While the moon glow glittered back
Dancing crimson along the ripples

—Omar Tate, June 5, 2019

INTRODUCTION

African Americans crave locally harvested, coast-to-coast, USDA Prime liberty, in all its bitter sweetness.

On June 19, 1865, more than two years after President Abraham Lincoln signed the Emancipation Proclamation, Major General Gordon Granger arrived in Galveston and issued General Order No. 3, informing the people of Texas that all enslaved people were now free. For the more than 250,000 enslaved Black Texans, the impact of the order was not immediate; some plantation owners withheld the information, delaying until after one more harvest season. But a year later, in 1866, unofficial Juneteenth celebrations began in Texas.

radually, Black people in other parts of the country embraced Juneteenth as the unofficial holiday commemorating the origin point of their American freedom. One hundred fifty-four years later, President Joseph R. Biden Jr. signed the Juneteenth National Independence Day Act. Among others at his side was Ms. Opal Lee, a Fort Worth, Texas–born nonagenarian and retired educator who had lobbied for the holiday to be recognized nationally, gathering more than 1.5 million signatures on her Juneteenth petition. Much like Martin Luther King Jr. Day, the nation's second national commemoration honoring the triumph of the African American experience became an institution with the stroke of the presidential pen. But the jubilation was mixed with trepidation, coming as it did amid troubling news of the increasing spread of COVID-19, new laws aimed at suppressing the Black vote, and the unrelenting community trauma resulting from the numerous killings of unarmed Black people, many at the hands of law enforcement officers. Black joy often emanates from Black sorrow, and so it has been with that small Texas tendril of freedom, which has continued to spread and strengthen.

In my own way, I have been a part of that spread. I've celebrated Juneteenth with the brightest people in the culinary space at a Soul Summit, a symposium founded by Toni Tipton-Martin in Austin, Texas, that celebrates the food history of African Americans; in New York, on a rooftop with my dearest friends; and in Georgia, tucked in the woods with humidity enveloping the guests. I've sat under my carport with chipped paint overhead and mosquitoes buzzing around a plethora of foil-covered foods: plump supermarket-bought Italian chicken sausages, buttery sweet pound cakes, pork ribs bathed in smoke and spices, and summery salads of heirloom tomatoes and roasted eggplant. I've hosted plated dinners with ceramic platters loaded down with whole roasted fish and summer bean salad, then carefully passed around a table draped in tea-dyed linens, accompanied by rum-spiked red punch. One year, I hosted a pop-up at Pelzer's Pretzels, a now-closed small-batch pretzel company, and served root beer floats drizzled with caramel and studded with pieces of Philadelphia-style pretzel, and another time I organized a neighborhood dinner and farm tour for Brownsville Community Culinary Center and Café. Guests feasted on Gullah Geechee classics like red rice and okra stew. Each of these celebrations was a time to block out the extraneous noise of the workaday world and feast on food and freedom. Through the years, Juneteenth has become my annual tradition, even when I am miles away from the places I call home.

Hosting all-day brunches and dinner parties is not something I was trained to do. It's a skill I picked up watching the deaconess board members at East Friendship Baptist Church (founded in 1882), respected women who led the church's outreach ministry. They masterfully organized family-style suppers of creamed corn, fried chicken, turnip greens, and cornbread for church anniversaries and youth days. Many of my best food memories are of those particular Sundays. By contrast, I spent my early adult years working for community-based health and environmental organizations. Later, I dabbled in selling real estate. While I always cooked for those closest to me, writing about food for a living was the furthest career choice from my mind. But I know the cadence of Black celebrations—the cheap fireworks, the whole pig barbecued for hours, the hot link sandwiches, sweet potato pie, red drinks, and dapper uncles gliding through the festivities, careful not to get dirt on their new 'gators. I felt a need to chronicle those cultural expressions. Increasingly, food publications and their editors have grown to see this need as well. So food has become both my life and my livelihood. These days I write "wandering victuals club" pieces for the *New York Times* Food section. I write about peach brandy for *Wine Enthusiast* and the magic of maple sugar for Epicurious. I develop recipes for *Food & Wine* and *EatingWell*. I now write about those things and much more, like where to eat Gullah food in Charleston, South Carolina; openings of New York City natural wine bars like The Fly; and how to make orange cocoa catfish.

But perhaps even more than my food writing, my Juneteenth gatherings have become the fullest and most personal of those cultural expressions. Everything from the music blaring from the speakers ('90s hip-hop, alt-R&B, Black classical music, and funk) to the signed Spike Lee posters and original Broderick Flanigan art on the walls to the fashions of the invited guests (sustainable and bent to high-low Black-owned fashion designers like Telfar and Tracy Reese with department store gear) is calibrated in such a way that even this leisurely gathering speaks to a day as important as it is tasty.

Watermelon & Red Birds is the first cookbook celebrating Juneteenth. It is meant to be a bridge between those traditional dishes of African American celebration and those flavors that I have come to know and appreciate as my culinary horizons have broadened. This book is not an attempt to capture the tastes and recipes of that 1866 Juneteenth celebration. This is a testament to where we are now. It's an attempt to synthesize all the places we've been, all the people we have come from, all the people we have become, and all the culinary ideas we have embraced. It's an attempt to fashion a Juneteenth celebration for the twenty-first century.

The title combines a native-born African fruit—watermelon—with the African American and Native American adage that red birds flying in sight are ancestors returning to spread beautiful luck. I wrote these recipes and stories as my contribution to a growing genre of Black cookbooks that centers creativity over tradition. Books that seek more to chart a future for African American cookery than to celebrate and record its richly deserving past. This is my declaration of independence from the traditional boundaries of so-called Southern food and soul food. It's my fulfillment of the dreams of those domestics, inventors, bakers, and bartenders who form the base of my family tree. It is my statement that we are free to fly.

When I wrote my first cookbook, *Up South*, I returned to Athens, Georgia, to ground myself. I did that again for this book. While I was writing, like clockwork and just as my mama would remind me as a kid, birds would appear at the exact moment when I needed their inspiration the most. And during solo weekend writing getaways in Charlotte, North Carolina; Pinpoint, Georgia; and Beaufort, South Carolina, I was reminded of what Black summer joy feels like: family barbecues and cookouts, Six Flags amusement park trips, Atlanta's Sweet Auburn Festival, seeded watermelons, Cross Colours T-shirts, peanut butter parfaits, Vacation Bible School brownies, recreation center cakewalks, and, of course, Juneteenth.

Like the Great Black Migration itself, Juneteenth traveled aboard trains and automobiles from its Texas birthplace to every state in the Union where Jim Crow was not the de facto governor. Daniel Vaughn writes in a 2015 *Texas Monthly* article about Juneteenth BBQ: "Barbecue wasn't the only item on the menu. The middle of June being the beginning of watermelon season in Texas, that also found a spot at the table. The *Galveston Daily News* reported on celebrations across the state in 1883 including one in San Antonio where 'twenty-three wagons loaded with watermelons . . . were destroyed with marvelous rapidity.' By 1933, the menu had been cemented per the *Dallas Morning News*. 'Watermelon, barbecue and red lemonade will be consumed in quantity.' "

There is no perfect city to celebrate Juneteenth; you don't have to be from the Lone Star State to experience it. Migrants in Oakland, California, and Milwaukee, Wisconsin, created the largest public Juneteenth festivals outside Texas; Milwaukee's public celebration dates back to 1971. It is fitting that Juneteenth celebrations not be confined to Texas. The Juneteenth theme of freedom delayed is one that recurs in American history, in every state. Even after emancipation, the passage of the Fifteenth Amendment in 1870 was required to nominally ensure that the right to vote wasn't denied to men on the basis of race. Poll taxes, grandfather clauses, lynchings, and other terrorist techniques were used throughout much of the nation to ensure that Black men wouldn't exercise this right. It wasn't until 1920 that women were allowed to vote. It wasn't until 1947 that Native Americans were given the right to vote. Asian Americans had to wait until passage of the McCarran-Walter Act (or Immigration and Nationality Act) in 1952. Not until the passage of the Voting Rights Act of 1965 did Black Americans gain federal protection against discrimination during elections.

This book is intended to be light with the pleasures of good food and heavy with the weight of history. Every morning, I stand at my altar and ask the Most High if she is pleased with how I'm moving through the world; do I reflect the goodness of my ancestors? On special occasions, when I'm slipping out of my clothes and jewelry, I wonder if I left bread crumbs for a future generation to follow. As my candlelight flickers, I hear, *Well done.* I know the red birds are out there, even in the dark.

HOW TO USE THIS COOKBOOK

My bedroom has a floor-to-ceiling bookshelf filled with titles written by Black authors. An Edna Lewis cookbook stack with all first editions and a Dr. Jessica B. Harris book tower with a signed *High on the Hog* **on top, and then a barbecue pile with Bobby Seale, Adrian Miller, Al Roker, and Rodney Scott. I've never been more elated about the wealth of authors telling their families' stories, sharing recipes from their travels in Paris, or being happily single (Klancy Miller's** *Cooking Solo* **and Vallery Lomas's** *Life Is What You Bake It***).**

My cookbooks follow me from the couch to the nightstand, desk, and kitchen at different times of the year. One day, I might be reading them. Another day, I might be cooking from them. On still another, I might be thumbing through their pages for inspiration. Bryant Terry's *Black Food* and Shannon Mustipher's *Tiki: Modern Tropical Cocktails* have dog-eared recipes, and Toni Tipton-Martin's *The Jemima Code* is sitting pretty. The pages of this cookbook are begging for indentations from nightlights and splatters of cake batter—my hope is that you read and cook.

The book begins with some resources to guide you as you read and cook. Chapters are organized to help you plan for your own celebrations. All the recipes can be doubled to accomodate a larger crowd.

I've included a few more resources here, including a nifty summer food pyramid (see page 16), so you can easily find the best ingredients to make these recipes for Juneteenth and more. Finally, I've listed brands from all across the US that are my favorite of the moment or that I've bought or used for many years. Some businesses are hyperlocal and require an in-person visit.

This isn't a tome dedicated to classic sweet potato pie, mac and cheese, and red velvet cake; instead, you'll find riffs off ingredients found on the traditional Black American family table. First come the "Red Drinks" to kick off the festivities, because they're a Juneteenth essential. The chapter has recipes for watermelon ginger beer and strawberry lemonade, both nonalcoholic large-batch beverages. I've provided instructions for cocktails with homemade syrups; there will be extra leftover, which is a good thing (they'll keep for several weeks in the fridge). The cocktails with homemade syrups require a Boston shaker and/or a bar spoon. If you have a fully stocked bar with gin, tequila, vodka, rum, and sparkling white wine, you're all set to make many libations. You'll see aromatic bitters (alcohol-based botanical infusions) mentioned in other cocktail recipes and in dessert dishes, too. I keep Angostura and Peychaud's bitters in my bar cabinet. Feel free to explore other brands.

"Festivals & Fairs" is my love letter to Americana, and you'll find festival foods here. "Cookout & BBQ" follows. The BBQ recipes are written for a charcoal grill or gas grill, and I've made the BBQ recipes easy enough for the novice cook, with exciting flavors that will make the master home cook pay attention. Next comes "Potato, Green & Fruit Salads," then desserts—in two chapters. Recipes for fruit desserts are written for fresh fruit, but frozen fruit can be substituted; just make sure the fruit is defrosted and all the juices are drained (I've made fruity drinks by adding that drained juice to seltzer for a terrific beverage—waste not, want not). In the last chapter, "Everyday Juneteenth," I share how comfort dishes can be part of a "24/7 and 365" self-care routine. I know for sure that the euphoric feeling of Juneteenth can be transferred to winter afternoons when dirty snow is covering your driveway. This mighty section is a reminder to choose joy in all we do.

Each of the book's eight chapters begins with an essay. These are a gateway to both American history and my celebrations. The words are meant to quench a thirst for a deeper dive into the Black cultural history that redefined communities. The reflections in the essays are an extension of my three decades of journaling about the experiences of living and growing here. The recipes follow.

JUNETEENTH GADGETS

In my first cookbook, *Up South*, I shared my essential tools and equipment—including knives. Except for replacing worn pots and pans, that list remains the same, and I hope you'll refer to it. In this cookbook, I shine a light on unique gadgets that make planning Juneteenth easier and direct you to use the right tools for each task—a cast-iron skillet isn't a must for every recipe, just the ones where I call for it.

 bet you have utensils that you use only once per year—for Friendsgiving, birthdays, Easter, Passover, Kwanzaa. Juneteenth needs gadgets, too. You'll find recipes in this book that need a specific tool. A snow cone maker is required. Smashed cubes of ice and fluffy bowls of perfectly shaved frozen water are two different things. The internet is an excellent resource for DIY hacks on pitting cherries, cutting spiral potatoes, and swirling funnel cake batter in hot oil. Still, I find using task-specific gadgets exhilarating when you have family around. Knowing he'll get to help impale the frankfurters on the wooden skewers is enough to send my kid rushing to the kitchen island for corn dog–making sessions. Watching an old friend who can't boil water get excited to make salad dressing because he'll get to use a unique shaker is a thrill. I call this "gadget joy."

I dreamed up this list because I needed a response to the question "What special tools should I buy to make your Juneteenth recipes?" More important, I discovered many incredible inventions while serving on the Museum of Food and Drink's advisory committee for an exhibit titled *African/American: Making the Nation's Table*, **which** increased my appreciation for the gadget department in places like Stock Culinary Goods (Providence, Rhode Island), Whisk (Brooklyn, New York), The Cook's Warehouse (Atlanta, Georgia), PW Short General Store (Savannah, Georgia), and HomeGoods. From the late 1800s into the 1900s, African American makers patented and tweaked the design of many standard kitchen tools. We'll find untold stories of grit and ingenuity in countertop or tool caddy machinery. Advances in the ice cream scoop and biscuit cutter changed the way Americans navigated kitchens. I cringe at the thought of paring down my gadget drawers because of this. More so, I love the rush from opening the "fun drawer" and picking up a tool that is so effective for the task at hand.

Metal and wooden skewers

I've used both, and each has its advantages and drawbacks, so pick either one. Wooden skewers require soaking in water before use, and they can't be cooked over high heat for too long. Metal skewers are sharper, so they allow for easier spearing. But unless you get flat ones, your chunks of meat or vegetables might spin around as you move the skewers.

Piston funnel

You need this tool for Juneteenth funnel cakes. I like that it helps control hand motion and creates pieces of circle dough art. Sure, you can achieve the same taste and shape without the thumb-triggered piston, but if you need a leg up, this is it.

Potato spiral cutter

Forget the hacks you might've seen on the internet and just buy this cutter. You'll get the perfect potato Slinky. Once you cut a few potatoes, you'll get the hang of it.

Crinkle fry potato cutter

French fries are my death row meal. I believe that each specific shape has its own personality and perfect application. Wavy shapes are perfect for cradling nacho-style toppings. Crinkle fries have more surface area than their straight cousins, so they are "it" for dipping, even into ice cream (try it!).

Cedar wood planks

Simple and easy. These wooden planks are a straightforward way to infuse flavor into food. Also, they assist with keeping delicate fish intact when it's being cooked on blazing-hot grill grates. The whole trout from the BBQ chapter (see page 118) holds together nicely on a cedar plank.

Grill basket

Seafood on the grill can be tricky; the high heat can rip flaky fish apart. A fish grill basket is a must-have tool for cooking foolproof fillets and whole fish and for presentation. I use a vegetable grill basket for my Fancy Mushrooms (page 138).

Salad dressing shaker

I'm a sucker for salad dressing shakers; I have a handful. They function largely as storage containers for me, but from time to time, I glance down at the recipes and proportions written on the bottle for dressing inspiration.

Corn zipper

Forget everything you've been taught and everything you've seen in YouTube tutorials. Just use this. A corn zipper gets the kernels off the cob quickly and easily. Lockrum Blue is responsible for speeding up the maize removal: he received a patent in 1884 for a handheld corn-shelling device.

Melon baller

Years ago, a melon baller appeared in my utensil drawer—I don't remember buying it. It was the perfect solution for carving fruit to decorate a cheese plate for my husband's art show opening.

Snow cone machine

There are lots of products on the market for making fluffy shaved ice for snow cones. The Cuisinart snow cone maker is what I use the most. It has a sleek look and tucks away in the cabinet easily. My friend and food editor Sara Bonisteel swears by the Little Snowie Max; I trust her recommendations. And Jenn de la Vega, a recipe developer and cookbook author, let me borrow her electric ice shaver. It takes up a ton of space, but it produces excellent snow cones (the best of the three options here, in my opinion).

Snow cone cups—paper

Functional and flimsy—the perfect words to describe this type of snow cone vessel. Keep a stack and double 'em up. These are a must for a large crowd.

Snow cone cups—plastic

I call this the luxury cone for icy treats. The plastic is more durable when you're adding booze. They are reusable and sturdy.

Ice pop molds

These are very inexpensive and take up little space. Pick your shape and your fruit or vegetable, add yogurt, and freeze.

Ice cream maker

I remember doing a lot of research before investing in my first ice cream machine. My first thought was to purchase an ice cream maker attachment for my KitchenAid stand mixer, but I decided on a Cuisinart frozen yogurt and ice cream maker with two freezer bowls. (I used a Whynter compressor-powered ice cream maker for the recipes, but it's a splurge, especially if you only make ice cream occasionally.)

Ice cream scoop

A Zeroll scoop, made with fluid inside the handle that heats up when scooping, is my preferred utensil for ice cream. But I still have and use my old trigger-mechanism scoop, too. Alfred L. Cralle is responsible for an 1896 patent for a trigger-operated one-handed ice cream scoop that he called the "ice cream mold and disher."

Pound cake pans

If you are a baker, you probably already have a 10-inch Bundt pan. But bear in mind, a Bundt pan with an ornate or unusual shape can add an aesthetic to your celebration that screams "special," even though putting cake batter in a fancy pan is no more difficult than putting it in a plain one.

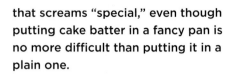

Waffle maker

Memories are bound to be big and bold when you have a waffler in the cabinet. I've gone through three versions, from a model without a temperature control to gas stovetop flippers to a hotel-style waffler. This is 100 percent an everyday Juneteenth gadget.

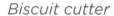

Biscuit cutter

All I've used are stainless-steel biscuit cutters, both round and square. I've been eyeing those wooden biscuit cutters. They look like pieces of art, with their heirloom-looking stains. Alexander P. Ashbourne was a Philadelphia-based inventor who patented a spring-loaded biscuit cutter, which created biscuits of a precise shape and size.

Cherry pitter

How does one remove the pits without a pitter? I have not a clue. (It seems that metal paper clips are one way—I'll pass.) Please just buy this and make eating tart cherries painless.

JUNETEENTH PANTRY

I've made sure the ingredients in this cookbook are accessible—the average supermarket will carry the items needed for these recipes. There are a few things that I'd recommend you keep in your pantry—salts, oils, vinegars, flours, and nuts.

I'll start with salt:

At any given moment, I have more than a half dozen varieties of salt on hand for cooking, but I stuck with three while testing this cookbook: kosher, flaky, and fine. Diamond Crystal kosher salt is used throughout the book; if you use Morton's kosher, please adjust by cutting the measurement in half (so, for example, if a recipe calls for 2 tablespoons kosher salt, use 1 tablespoon of Morton's). Flaky salt is what I use for finishing dishes, and Maldon, Bulls Bay Saltworks, J.Q. Dickinson Salt-Works, and Jacobsen Salt Co. are the brands I use the most. For recipes that call for

a salt that dissolves quickly but has a more pronounced flavor than regular table salt, I use fine sea salt.

Now, on the oils and vinegars:

Costco's Kirkland Signature (or any store brand) and California Olive Ranch are the olive oils I reach for for everyday uses; any inexpensive olive oil works fine for cooking. Typically, for dishes that don't involve heating olive oil on the stove or in the oven, I splurge on expensive high-quality extra-virgin olive oil—it's perfect for finishing salads and grains. When I'm frying, peanut oil is a must. It ensures a golden brown outside on food, and shouldn't set off your smoke alarm when heated to the right temperature. For individuals with nut allergies, use vegetable oil instead. You can strain your frying oil and reuse it: Let the oil cool completely, then, using a double strainer and a funnel, pour the oil into a clean airtight container and seal. Store in a dark, cool place and use the next time you fry.

Some cooks will gasp at the five vinegar varieties present throughout this cookbook. As a master home cook, I tend to keep apple cider, white distilled, balsamic (the real good stuff like Sadel, made in Modena, Italy), red wine, sherry, rice, and many more tiny regional US brands. Please don't be frightened if it's your first time exploring outside the apple cider and white varieties. Feel free to play around and substitute but keep in mind the nuances and subtleties. O Olive Oil & Vinegars is a California brand easily found on supermarket shelves; I recommend their product for premium vinegar newbies.

Moving along to flours:

All-purpose, cake, buckwheat, and rye flours are used in various recipes in this book. Except for the all-purpose flour, I encourage you to buy specialty flours in small quantities and store them in an airtight bag in the freezer, labeled and dated. I feel the same about cornmeal. The key to superior cornbread, whether adding chives, red onions, or peppers, is good cornmeal. I buy nonenriched products from local millers. My go-tos are DaySpring Farms, Anson Mills, and Marsh Hen Mill. Freshness is key, so proper storage is crucial. Like flour, I keep my cornmeal in an airtight bag in the freezer, labeled and dated.

The same instructions apply to nuts:

Pecans, peanuts, Brazil nuts, walnuts, almonds, pistachios—buy the best your money can afford and store in the freezer to preserve freshness.

JUNETEENTH FOOD PYRAMID

I'm a fixture at the Fort Greene and Grand Army Plaza Greenmarkets in New York City, the Athens Farmers Market in Georgia, and any other place I go with local farmers corralled in one location (like the Port Royal Farmers Market in South Carolina and the Foothills Farmers Market in Shelby, North Carolina), so I know how daunting it can be to shop surrounded by such abundance. This pyramid will help.

Figs
Plums
Peaches
Mangoes
Apricots
Cherries
Strawberries
Watermelon
Cantaloupe
Nectarines
Blueberries

Rhubarb
Garlic
Cucumber
Radishes
Carrots
Snap Peas
Turnips

Edible Flowers
Chocolate Mint
Oregano
Basil
Chamomile

BIPOC-OWNED BRANDS

I know a lot of people reach for seasoned salt before they put the food in the pan and they reach for the Texas Pete as soon as the food hits the plate. But I've found a few small-batch artisanal seasonings that hit the taste buds in new and different ways.

Red Boat Fish Sauce, the fermented fish umami splash sprinkled throughout these pages, is one of these brands. Husband-and-wife duo Michael and Shyretha Sheats cooked and tended the bar, respectively, at Atlanta's Staplehouse. They also created The Plate Sale, a food business inspired by the tradition of selling "plates" or suppers for fund-raisers. Among the items they sell is a great hot sauce with a provocative name: Fug Widit. Michael Twitty is best known as a culinary historian, but he has joined forces with Spice Tribe to create a line of seasonings named after his James Beard Award–winning book *The Cooking Gene*. Lefty's Spices is a Maryland company that makes barbecue sauce. But my favorite Lefty's product is their Fish N' Chicken Mix for frying. As Psyche Williams-Forson details in her book *Building Houses out of Chicken Legs: Black Women, Food, and Power*, food entrepreneurship has been a lifeline for African Americans for centuries. Thanks to online ordering and national word of mouth, some of these small local businesses have been able to build strong national followings. I count myself lucky to be alive in an era when they are as close as my internet connection.

I'd die on a hill for these (primarily Black-owned and/or POC-owned) food brands. They are all quality products, and, in the spirit of Juneteenth, their very existence is a testament to the progress we've made.

Uncle Nitty's Herbs and Spices

Hot N Saucy

Diaspora Co.

Meadows and More

The Cooking Gene Spice Collection From Spice Tribe

SpiceWalla

Capital City Mambo Sauce

G Hughes Sugar-Free BBQ Sauce

Red Boat Fish Sauce

Lefty's Fish N' Chicken Mix

Trade Street Jam Co.

Janie Q Provisions

The Plate Sale

Tall Grass Food Box

Caribe United Farm

Yolélé

Me & the Bees Lemonade

La Newyorkina

Red Bay Coffee

Middleton Made Knives

Gastronomical

Mouton Noir Wines

McBride Sisters Wine Collection

Uncle Nearest Premium Whiskey

Deleon Tequila

Harlem Brewing Company

Daleview Biscuits and Beer

Ten to One Rum

Orange Peel Bakery

SPICE BLENDS, HOT SAUCES & PICKLED THINGS

SPICE BLENDS, HOT SAUCES & PICKLED THINGS

Some of the most common questions I receive from novice and experienced cooks alike are about adding flavor with seasoning blends, dashes of sauces, and spoonfuls of vinegary vegetables. I answer the spice-and-sauce question in two parts: I make my own blends, but my cabinets and counter are filled with small-batch specialty products like single-origin nutmeg from Diaspora Co., mambo sauce from Capital City, and smoked yellow peach jam from Trade Street Jam Co.

f course, in families that are the most serious about their culinary traditions, spice blends and hot sauce recipes often get passed down. I wasn't fortunate enough to inherit such wealth. But I do love the idea that in addition to these premade options, I can create my own seasonings to help give my food a uniquely consistent flavor. These recipes might well be the most valuable things my young son will inherit from me.

I use a spice grinder to make my peppercorn rub. Before I grind or smash seeds, nuts, or whole spices for blends, I toast them. In a small skillet, I heat ingredients like whole fennel seeds over medium-low heat for 3 minutes, or until fragrant. Be sure not to burn the spices, and let them cool down before grinding and mixing with other ground spices.

For the other salts and rubs and the fry mix, combine all the ingredients in a medium bowl with a small wooden spoon; mix well until everything is evenly distributed. Be sure to label your mixes with the date you made them, because while they won't spoil, they will lose their potency over time.

The sauces require a heavy saucepan with a lid. Once made, they can be stored in an airtight container in the fridge; I've noted the shelf life in each recipe. I've paired sauces like the rhubarb BBQ sauce with meatless baked beans (see page 114), but they also work well with pork ribs (see page 139), and the green garlic chimichurri is perfect for more than lamb chops (see page 128)—try it with rib eye (see page 123), too. I encourage mixing and matching sauces for your celebration dishes and everyday meals.

Throughout the cookbook, I'll direct you to use these staples. Buy store-bought mixes, spice blends, or hot sauces if you're in a crunch. But you should try to make your own, complete with your personal variations, too. Let the circle be unbroken for the next generation.

ALL-PURPOSE SEASONING

MAKES 2 SCANT CUPS

This seasoning is a dry rub, although "dry rub" is something of a misnomer. You don't "rub" this into meat the way a massage therapist rubs oil into your skin. You do sprinkle it generously, though. And once it cooks into the meat, the flavors sing.

1 cup packed dark brown sugar

6 tablespoons kosher salt

2 tablespoons fresh oregano

4 teaspoons sweet paprika

4 teaspoons cumin seed

2 teaspoons garlic powder

2 teaspoons onion powder

1 teaspoon freshly ground black pepper

Combine the brown sugar, salt, oregano, paprika, cumin seed, garlic powder, onion powder, and pepper in a medium bowl. Stir using a wooden spoon until well combined. Store in an airtight container in a cool, dry place for several months.

LEMON PEPPER SEASONING

MAKES 2 CUPS

I know. When you read "lemon pepper," you assume there are only two ingredients. But trust me, while the lemon and pepper dominate this spice blend, the other ingredients complement them beautifully.

1 cup lemon zest (from about 16 lemons)

½ cup whole black peppercorns

2 tablespoons plus 2 teaspoons kosher salt

5 tablespoons plus 1 teaspoon onion powder

2 tablespoons plus 2 teaspoons garlic powder

Preheat the oven to 200ºF. Spread the lemon zest evenly over a baking sheet. Toast the zest in the oven for 5 to 7 minutes, until dried out. Stir the zest using a spatula to break up any clumps. Return the baking sheet to the oven and turn the oven off. Leave the zest in the warm oven to cool completely and continue to dry out.

Meanwhile, place the peppercorns and the salt in a spice grinder and grind until the peppercorns are coarsely chopped. Transfer the peppercorn mixture to a small bowl and add the dried lemon zest, onion powder, and garlic powder. Mix to combine using a wooden spoon. Store in an airtight container in a cool, dry place for several months.

SWEET POTATO SEASONING

MAKES 2 CUPS

In this cookbook, this seasoning is for a whole sweet potato fried in fat (see page 94). However, it also works on a beautifully baked orange spud or sprinkled over a breakfast sweet potato hash with a fried egg. I credit my friend Jamie Swofford, farmer and founder of Old North Shrub, for putting me onto the fennel-seeds-and-sweet-potato game.

¾ cup plus 2 tablespoons fennel seeds

1⅓ cups fresh thyme leaves

¼ cup plus 3 tablespoons kosher salt

3 tablespoons plus 2 teaspoons hot paprika

In a small bowl, combine the fennel seeds, thyme, salt, and paprika. Stir using a wooden spoon until well combined. Store in an airtight container in a cool, dry place for several months.

CHILI POWDER

MAKES 2 CUPS

A well-stocked pantry will have all the goods to make chili powder from scratch. One day, I started making my own chili powder because I needed a few teaspoons more for my winter chili. It's perfectly fine to use whole cumin and coriander seeds. Remember to toast before grinding. (½ tablespoon of whole coriander equals 1 tablespoon ground. For the cumin seeds, 1 tablespoon equals about ¾ tablespoon ground.)

½ cup smoked paprika or ground chile (like ancho or chipotle)

6 tablespoons ground cumin

6 tablespoons garlic powder

3 tablespoons dried oregano

2 tablespoons cayenne pepper

2 tablespoons onion powder

1 tablespoon ground coriander

1 tablespoon unsweetened cocoa powder

In a small bowl, combine the paprika, cumin, garlic powder, oregano, cayenne, onion powder, coriander, and cocoa powder. Stir using a wooden spoon until well combined. Store in an airtight container in a cool, dry place for several months.

CHICKEN SALT

MAKES 2 CUPS

Chicken plays such an important role in world cuisine in general, and in African American cuisine in particular, that I think it deserves its own special salt. Of course, you can feel free to sprinkle this on pork or beef or any other food you think it would taste good on.

1 cup plus 2 tablespoons kosher salt

¼ cup celery seed

¼ cup cumin seed

¼ cup onion powder

Combine the salt, celery seed, cumin seed, and onion powder in a medium bowl. Stir using a wooden spoon until well combined. Store in an airtight container at room temperature for several months.

CITRUS VERBENA SALT

MAKES 2 CUPS

Maldon sea salt is the perfect salt for finishing a dish because its small flakes add a slight crunchiness. But for some next-level salt with more flavor, try these additions. Sesame, or benne (the term enslaved Africans most likely brought from West Africa's Bantu), is a seed with notes of brown butter and warm honey. The fennel, lemon verbena, and cocoa are all familiar ingredients that are seldom used in concert to flavor savory dishes, where they play surprisingly well together. If you can't find fresh lemon verbena, feel free to substitute fresh or dried chamomile flowers, or lemon zest or dried lemon peel.

⅓ cup benne seeds

1 cup flaky salt

1 cup fresh lemon verbena blossoms

2 tablespoons plus 2 teaspoons fennel seeds

4 teaspoons unsweetened cocoa powder

Combine the benne seeds, salt, lemon verbena blossoms, fennel seeds, and cocoa powder in a small bowl. Stir well with a wooden spoon to combine. Store in an airtight container in a cool, dry place for several months.

PEPPERCORN RUB

MAKES 2 CUPS

This blend of peppercorns and other spices adds deep flavor without adding overpowering heat. Black peppercorns you likely know well. Green peppercorns are just unripe black peppercorns and tend to be milder than their darker cousins. Pink peppercorns are not really peppercorns at all. They come from a totally different plant. But blended together and cut slightly with paprika and mustard seeds, they render a rounded heat to anything you add them to.

½ cup whole black peppercorns

¼ cup whole green peppercorns

½ cup whole pink peppercorns

¼ cup kosher salt

1 tablespoon sweet paprika

1 tablespoon whole mustard seeds

Combine the black, green, and pink peppercorns, salt, paprika, and mustard seeds in a medium bowl. Stir using a wooden spoon until well combined. Store in an airtight container in a cool, dry place for several months.

DUKKAH

MAKES 2 CUPS

You might be wondering why this North African nut blend is included here. Traditionally, dukkah is served with olive oil. Then, bread or vegetables are dipped in the oil and seasoning. It seems out of place because the majority of the recipes in this cookbook are classic American recipes, but the inspiration *is* a classic American recipe. I was looking for something that, when pressed into thick-cut pieces of meat, like a pork chop or drumstick, would look like that Shake 'n Bake mix.

⅔ cup Brazil nuts

⅓ cup raw pecans

⅓ cup raw peanuts

⅓ cup sesame seeds

4 teaspoons fennel seeds

2¾ teaspoons cumin seeds

2¾ teaspoons coriander seeds

1¼ teaspoons kosher salt

¾ teaspoon cayenne pepper

In a small dry skillet, toast the Brazil nuts, pecans, and peanuts over medium-high heat, stirring frequently, until toasted and nutty in fragrance, 2 to 3 minutes. Transfer to a plate to cool.

In the same skillet, toast the sesame, fennel, cumin, and coriander seeds over medium heat until fragrant, 30 seconds to 1 minute. Transfer the seeds to a plate and allow to cool.

Transfer the cooled nuts to a food processor or a mortar and pulse or crush the nuts a few times with the pestle to break up any big pieces. Add the cooled seeds and pulse or crush until the mixture has a rough, rocky texture. Do not overprocess or blend into a paste. Transfer the mixture to a medium bowl and stir in the salt and cayenne. Store in an airtight container in a cool, dry place for several months.

FISH FRY MIX

MAKES 2 CUPS

You're probably already using most of the ingredients in this mix when you fry your fish, but three may surprise: The baking powder helps lend extra crisp to the crust. The amount of sugar here is enough to enhance the flavor without creating an obvious sweetness. And the nutritional yeast adds a great burst of umami flavor.

1⅓ cups yellow cornmeal

⅔ cup all-purpose flour

2½ teaspoons nutritional yeast

2 teaspoons kosher salt

1¼ teaspoons sugar

¾ teaspoon baking powder

¾ teaspoon red pepper flakes

¾ teaspoon freshly ground black pepper

1¼ teaspoons dried lemon peel, or
1¼ tablespoons lemon zest (optional)

Combine the cornmeal, flour, nutritional yeast, salt, sugar, baking powder, red pepper flakes, black pepper, and lemon peel (if using) in a medium bowl. Stir using a wooden spoon until well combined. Store in an airtight container in a cool, dry place for several months.

FIG VINEGAR BBQ SAUCE

MAKES 4 SCANT CUPS

This is a play on the classic Carolina vinegar-based sauce. Lots of vinegar and a hint of tomatoes. After being gifted fresh figs from Rachel Watkins, an avid gardener, backyard chicken keeper, and bookshop manager, I needed to use up the summer bounty. Since figs are a superb natural sugar substitute, I used them here instead of the brown sugar found in most traditional versions of the sauce.

2 cups apple cider vinegar

½ cup water

2 tablespoons tomato paste

1 cup fresh figs, sliced in half

2 tablespoons kosher salt

1 tablespoon freshly ground black pepper

1 tablespoon red pepper flakes

Combine the vinegar, water, tomato paste, figs, salt, black pepper, and red pepper flakes in a clean jar. Place a lid on the jar and shake until well combined. Store in the jar in the refrigerator for 3 to 4 days.

RHUBARB BBQ SAUCE

MAKES 4½ CUPS

When most people hear "rhubarb," they expect the word "pie" to follow shortly. But the savory tartness of rhubarb stalks complements the vinegar that is a staple of even the sweetest barbecue sauces. The sugars and such here balance out that tartness nicely.

3 tablespoons "everyday" olive oil

2 cups chopped rhubarb

1 large sweet onion, chopped

6 garlic cloves, sliced

3½ cups tomato puree

1⅓ cups water

½ cup plus 2 tablespoons unsulfured molasses

½ cup apple cider vinegar

¼ cup packed dark brown sugar

2½ teaspoons kosher salt

1 teaspoon chili powder

1 teaspoon red pepper flakes

½ teaspoon freshly ground black pepper

1 teaspoon ground mustard

½ teaspoon freshly grated nutmeg

3½ tablespoons unsalted butter, sliced

In a large saucepan, heat the olive oil over medium heat. Add the rhubarb, onion, and garlic and cook until softened, 4 to 6 minutes. Add the tomato puree, water, molasses, vinegar, brown sugar, salt, chili powder, red pepper flakes, black pepper, ground mustard, and nutmeg and stir to combine using a spatula. Bring the mixture to a boil, then reduce the heat to low to maintain a simmer and cook for 30 to 40 minutes, until thickened and reduced by almost half to about 4 cups. Stir in the butter and allow it to melt completely. Remove the sauce from the heat and allow to cool for at least 10 minutes.

Using a ladle, transfer the sauce to a blender or place an immersion blender in the saucepan and blend until smooth, scraping down the sides as needed. Allow the sauce to cool completely. Store in an airtight container in the refrigerator for up to 1 week.

TIP: If you're using a whole nutmeg in the shell—like those sold by Diaspora Co.—first crack the shell and peel it away to remove the seed inside, then grate the seed into a powder using a Microplane or other grater. Just grate what you need; store the remaining portion of the seed in an airtight container.

PEACH & MOLASSES SAUCE

MAKES 1 CUP

Listen—I'm going to let you in on a secret. As much as I love to pick fruit, as much as I love to cook, I haven't mastered making jam. So this is one of the times when I rely on makers who are better than I am. This sauce is so amazing on chicken thighs (see page 121) and chicken breasts. It's special enough for your Juneteenth celebration, but it's so delicious, it's on my weekly rotation. Almost any fruit jam works, too, if peach isn't your thing.

1 cup peach jam

1 cup water

½ cup unsulfured molasses

2 tablespoons apple cider vinegar

¼ cup tomato paste

2 tablespoons soy sauce

2 tablespoons coriander seeds, crushed

2 tablespoons ground mustard

1 teaspoon salt

In a small saucepan, combine the peach jam, water, molasses, and vinegar and bring to a boil over medium-high heat, stirring occasionally to combine. Once boiling, reduce the heat to medium-low and whisk in the tomato paste, soy sauce, coriander, ground mustard, and salt. Simmer for 6 to 8 minutes, until thickened; the sauce should be reduced to about 1 cup. Store in an airtight container in the refrigerator for 3 to 4 days.

ROMESCO

MAKES 2 CUPS

Red peppers join the canon of red vegetables and fruits. Stale or toasted bread is sometimes added to romesco, or red pepper sauce, for thickness. My version omits that ingredient. It's terrific on fish—I suggest the salmon on page 254.

1 large tomato, halved crosswise

1 large red bell pepper, halved and seeded

⅓ cup whole almonds

1 garlic clove, peeled

1¼ teaspoons smoked paprika

1¼ teaspoons kosher salt

1 tablespoon fresh lemon juice

1 tablespoon red wine vinegar

⅓ cup extra-virgin olive oil

Position the top rack of the oven 6 inches away from the broiler heat element and preheat the broiler to high. Line a baking sheet with foil.

Score an X into the skin on the top and bottom of the tomato. Place the tomato and bell pepper cut-side down on the prepared baking sheet. Broil for 8 to 10 minutes, until the skins have blistered. Using a pair of tongs, flip the pepper and tomato halves and broil for 5 to 8 minutes more, until the edges blacken. Remove the vegetables from the oven. Allow the vegetables to cool until easy enough to handle, then peel them and set the flesh aside.

In a food processor, pulse the almonds until they're coarsely chopped. Add the peeled bell pepper and tomato, the garlic, paprika, and salt. Process until smooth. Scrape down the sides of the food processor with a spatula.

With the motor running, slowly add the lemon juice, vinegar, and olive oil and process until fully blended. Store in an airtight container in the refrigerator for 3 to 4 days.

NAT'S RED HOT SAUCE

MAKES 2 CUPS

The past few years, I've grown obsessed with hot sauces. I'm not a believer that everything needs hot sauce and that each bottle must be fiery. This blend is what I enjoy now. A version of this sauce comes from my recipe in *The Last O.G. Cookbook*, but I continue to tweak the variety of chiles and other ingredients to finish the sauce.

1 pound fresh chiles, stemmed and chopped

3 tablespoons kosher salt

1 teaspoon vegetable oil

2 garlic cloves, minced

1 medium yellow onion, chopped

2 medium tomatoes, chopped

1 cup distilled white vinegar

2 tablespoons American whiskey

1 tablespoon honey

Mix the chiles and salt in a jar and cover. Let sit at room temperature for 8 hours or up to a full day.

In a medium-size saucepan, heat the oil over medium heat. Add the garlic and cook, stirring, for 1 to 2 minutes, until fragrant. Add the onion and tomatoes and cook for about 5 minutes, until soft. Remove from the heat and let cool for 10 minutes.

Transfer the tomato mixture and the chiles to a blender or food processor. Pulse a few times, then blend for 2 minutes, or until smooth. Stir in the vinegar, whiskey, and honey and blend to incorporate.

Using a double strainer and a funnel, pour the hot sauce into a jar or bottle and seal. Store in the refrigerator for up to a few weeks.

SALSA VERDE

MAKES 2 CUPS

In this cookbook, I recommend you use this salsa verde on Chorizo–Corn Chip Nachos (page 100). But I also treat salsa verde like a hot sauce, and add it to a Late-Night Steak Tostada (page 125) and more.

10 ounces tomatillos, husks removed, rinsed well

1 serrano pepper, stemmed

2 tablespoons coarsely chopped white onion

2 garlic cloves, peeled

⅔ cup fresh cilantro stems, coarsely chopped

2 tablespoons plus 2 teaspoons fresh lime juice

1¼ teaspoons kosher salt

Using heat-resistant tongs, hold a tomatillo directly over the flame of a gas stovetop burner, turning it every 30 seconds, until charred on all sides. Set aside and repeat with the remaining tomatillos and the serrano pepper; since the serrano is small, you may not need to turn it to char all sides. (If you have an electric stove, you'll need to use the broiler to char the tomatillos and serrano instead: Set the broiler to low and place the tomatillos and serrano on a small baking sheet. Broil for 30 seconds on each side, using heat-resistant tongs to flip them as they char.) Place the charred tomatillos and serrano in a large bowl and let cool until easy to handle.

Remove the stems of the tomatillos and coarsely chop the tomatillos and serrano. Transfer to a food processor or a high-speed blender. Add the onion, garlic, cilantro stems, lime juice, and salt. Process until smooth. Store in an airtight container in the refrigerator for 3 to 4 days.

HARISSA

MAKES 2 CUPS

A North Carolina farmer friend visiting New York gave me a hostess gift—homemade fermented harissa. He recommended I use it just like hot sauce. I wanted to create my own version here. I'll give you the same advice: use this just like hot sauce on a Late-Night Steak Tostada (page 125) and on the Beef Ribs (page 131).

2 poblano peppers

2 fresh red chiles

4 garlic cloves, coarsely chopped

2 teaspoons kosher salt

2 teaspoons coriander seeds

1 tablespoon cumin seeds

1 teaspoon caraway seeds

1 teaspoon smoked paprika

2 roasted red peppers

2 tablespoons fresh lemon juice

1 tablespoon tomato paste

½ cup extra-virgin olive oil

Using heat-resistant tongs, hold a poblano directly over the flame of a gas stovetop burner for 30 seconds on each side, until charred. Set aside and repeat with the remaining poblano and the red chiles. (If you have an electric stove, you'll need to use the broiler to char the peppers instead: Set the broiler to low and place the poblanos and chiles on a small baking sheet. Broil for 30 seconds on each side, using heat-resistant tongs to flip the peppers as they char.) Let cool.

Remove the stems, seeds, and white pith of the poblanos and red chiles and coarsely chop the flesh. Combine the poblanos, red chiles, garlic, and salt in a clean jar or plastic container. Cover and set aside to ferment at room temperature for at least 24 hours.

In a small dry skillet, toast the coriander, cumin, and caraway seeds over medium-low heat for 1 to 2 minutes, until fragrant. Transfer to a small plate and let cool, then grind the cooled spices using a mortar and pestle or a spice grinder.

Transfer the fermented poblano-chile mixture to a food processor and add the roasted red peppers, lemon juice, tomato paste, and spice mixture and process to combine. Add ¼ cup of olive oil and process until smooth, scraping down the sides to mix in larger pieces.

Transfer the harissa to a jar or plastic container and top off with the remaining ¼ cup olive oil. Store in an airtight container in the refrigerator for up to a few weeks.

GREEN GARLIC CHIMICHURRI

MAKES 2 CUPS

I know, I know: another sauce. But I promise you, this chimichurri is terrific on lamb chops (see page 128). Try it on pork chops or steak, too, and you'll be happy.

6 tablespoons coarsely chopped green garlic, or 6 garlic cloves, coarsely chopped

¾ cup fresh parsley leaves and stems, coarsely chopped

¾ cup fresh cilantro leaves and stems, coarsely chopped

1 fresh red chile, stemmed, seeded, and coarsely chopped

1 tablespoon plus 2 teaspoons fresh oregano leaves

3 tablespoons red wine vinegar

1½ cups extra-virgin olive oil

¾ teaspoon kosher salt

¾ teaspoon freshly ground black pepper

In a food processor, combine the garlic, parsley, cilantro, red chile, and oregano and pulse. Add the vinegar and, with the motor running, slowly pour in the olive oil. Use a rubber spatula to scrape down the sides and process until smooth. Stir in the salt and pepper and adjust the seasoning to your taste. Store in an airtight container in the refrigerator for 3 to 4 days.

QUICK-PICKLES

A handful of pickled carrots atop cheesy, creamy nachos adds tang and crunch. A side of pickled onions with a plate of beef ribs cuts through the fat. What I know for sure is that pickled vegetables (and fruit!) are essential for outdoor eating and everyday eating. They provide contrast, in terms of taste, texture, and more. You need a crunchy, salty, vinegary condiment, with a dash of sweetness, to brighten up your salads, BBQ, and, believe it or not, even your cocktails (see pages 70 and 73).

There are a few methods for pickling vegetables—this is the quick pickling method, which requires only brine and refrigeration. These quick pickles don't last months in your fridge, but I don't think they should: when you put pickled onions, peppers, blueberries, and more on your Juneteenth table, they are going to go fast, so I don't recommend you spend too much time on them. Make them quick because they go quick.

These are the quick-pickles on my Juneteenth table.

BLUEBERRIES

MAKES 1 CUP

1 cup blueberries

1 cup rice vinegar

½ cup water

3 bay leaves

2 teaspoons kosher salt

4 teaspoons sugar

2 strips grapefruit peel

Place the blueberries in a clean heatproof jar. Combine the vinegar, water, bay leaves, salt, sugar, and grapefruit peel in a small saucepan. Bring to a boil over medium heat and cook just until the sugar is dissolved. Pour the hot liquid over the blueberries and allow to cool to room temperature. Seal the jar with a lid and store in the refrigerator for up to a few weeks.

SQUASH SPEARS

MAKES 4 SPEARS

1 yellow squash, quartered

1 small shallot, sliced into rings

2 large garlic cloves, smashed and peeled

1 cup apple cider vinegar

¼ cup water

2 tablespoons kosher salt

2 tablespoons sugar

½ teaspoon coriander seeds

½ teaspoon red pepper flakes

2 teaspoons grainy mustard

Place the squash, shallot, and garlic in a clean heatproof jar. Combine the vinegar, water, salt, sugar, coriander seeds, red pepper flakes, and mustard in a small saucepan. Bring to a boil over medium-high heat and cook until the sugar has dissolved. Pour the hot liquid over the vegetables and allow to cool to room temperature. Seal the jar with a lid and store in the refrigerator for up to a few weeks.

BANANA PEPPERS

MAKES 1 CUP

1 cup sliced banana peppers (cut into rings; stemmed before slicing)

¾ cup apple cider vinegar

¼ cup water

1 tablespoon kosher salt

1 tablespoon sugar

½ teaspoon mustard seed

¼ teaspoon celery seed

Place the banana peppers in a clean heatproof jar. Combine the vinegar, water, salt, sugar, mustard seed, and celery seed in a small saucepan. Bring to a boil over medium-high heat and cook until the sugar is dissolved. Pour the hot liquid over the banana peppers and allow to cool to room temperature. Seal the jar with a lid and store in the refrigerator for up to a few weeks.

PURPLE CARROTS

MAKES 1 CUP

1 cup thinly sliced (⅛ inch thick) purple carrots

½ cup water

½ cup white vinegar

½ teaspoon whole black peppercorns

1 teaspoon coarse salt

2 tablespoons sugar

1 bay leaf

2 garlic cloves, thinly sliced

Place the carrot slices in a clean heatproof jar. Combine the water, vinegar, peppercorns, salt, sugar, and bay leaf in a small saucepan. Bring to a boil over medium-high heat and cook until the sugar is dissolved, 2 to 3 minutes, adding the garlic during the last 30 seconds. Pour the hot liquid over the carrots and allow to cool to room temperature. Seal the jar with a lid and store in the refrigerator for up to a few weeks.

RED ONIONS

MAKES 1 CUP

1 small red onion, thinly sliced

1 cup apple cider vinegar

½ cup water

2 bay leaves

4 teaspoons sugar

2 teaspoons kosher salt

2 strips of grapefruit peel (optional)

Place the onion slices in a clean heatproof jar. Combine the vinegar, water, bay leaves, sugar, salt, and grapefruit peel (if using) in a small saucepan. Bring to a boil over medium-high heat and cook until the sugar is dissolved. Pour the hot liquid over the onions and allow to cool to room temperature. Seal the jar with a lid and store in the refrigerator for up to a few weeks.

MENU PLANNING

If you're getting ready to plan your Juneteenth celebration, first things first:

Set your menu.

Create your shopping list.

Figure out what can be made ahead.

And use your judgment here. Pickles, sauces, and salad dressings can be made the day before. Some salads can be, too—for example, I like to prepare Crab & Egg Salad or Summer Peas, Green Beans & Corn Salad then, too.

There's more you can do that day.

Prep your Victory Chicken Burgers. Season your meat—beef ribs, rib eye steak, pork ribs, pork chops, lamb chops, and chicken thighs, too. Prep your Meatless Baked Beans.

Make sure you've assigned the potato salad to the Potato Salad Queen, whoever that is to you. Make sure you ask your favorite uncle to bring the vodka for the Sweet Potato Spritz. Make sure you've shared the recipe for Strawberry & Black Pepper Slab Pie with your young cousin, the aspiring baker.

I'm playing recipe matchmaker here. These combinations are suggestions. I tend to plan big menus and then eliminate or add sides the day of, based on time constraints, sometimes lack of ingredients, and/or extra guests. By all means, do what excites you but do choose a red drink and one showstopper for each menu. My general rule is that guests need two knockout dishes to remember the details from a gathering.

Happy Hour

Sweet Potato Spritz (page 69)

Crab & Egg Salad (page 159)

Broiler Salmon with Romesco
(page 254)

Blueberry & Beef Puff Pies (page 222)

Cantaloupe & Feta (page 163)

Shoebox Lunch

Rodeo Turkey Legs (page 105)

Yellow Squash & Cheddar Biscuits
(page 249)

Summer Peas, Green Beans & Corn
Salad (page 157)

Strawberry Hand Pies (page 203)

Radish & Ginger Pound Cake
(page 213)

Ice Cream Social

Honey Vanilla Ice Cream (page 185)

Corn Ice Cream Sandwiches (page 187)

Dairy-Free Chocolate Sorbet
(page 178)

Strawberry & Black Pepper Slab Pie
(page 207)

Rhubarb Compote (page 179)

Roasted Nectarine Sundae (page 183)

Pitted Fresh Cherries

Pistachio Brittle (page 186)

Whipped Cream

Fresh Mint

The Cookout

Hot Links (see page 127)

Beef Ribs with Harissa (page 131)

Victory Chicken Burgers (page 137)

Southern-ish Potato Salad (page 148)

Meatless Baked Beans (page 114)

Moscato Pound Cake (page 219)

Fanfare

Beer-Battered Shrimp (page 96)

Corn Dogs (page 87)

Tornado Sweet Potatoes (page 94)

Funnel Cake with Apple Topping
(page 82)

RED DRINKS

RED DRINKS

At Juneteenth, the official beverage is the "red drink"—red soda, red Kool-Aid, or red punch. The tradition of red drinks began mostly with the parts of two plants: the kola nuts, a seed of the cola plant, and hibiscus pod, the innermost part of the roselle flower. West African culture came to the US with the transatlantic slave trade, and so the drinking tradition of seeds steeped in water became incised into Black people's DNA. I keep a dried kola nut on my altar to honor our connection to Benin, to Negril, to Sapelo and Galveston Islands, year-round.

n his book *Soul Food: The Surprising Story of an American Cuisine, One Plate at a Time*, **food scholar and James Beard Award winner Adrian Miller** dedicates a section to red drinks. He writes, "Red drinks were plentiful in the plantation Big House. Antebellum southern cookbooks are replete with recipes for homemade cherry, raspberry, and strawberry liqueurs, syrups, and vinegars, kept on hand to color a wide range of hard and soft drinks." The drink's color, and aura, is paramount. It's visually bold, calling attention to itself as if to declare its own freedom from plain water or pale lemonade.

At least one ruby beverage must be consumed on Juneteenth. Whether it's a scarlet-colored margarita or watermelon lemonade, red drinks are a sultry bolster in a pitcher. You pour a cup: the condensation hits your fingers and aids in throwing your hands in the air from side to side. DJ Jazzy Jeff and The Fresh Prince's "Summertime" is bouncing throughout the room and getting you up from your seat to hug the person you haven't laid eyes on in forever (never putting down your cup). After a few sips, you can feel the spirit of a distant friend; bright lipstick stains on another glass remind you of hers.

After shaking a marigold sour and pouring it into a bone-cold vessel, I lean into my lacquered white dining table. I now have the courage to start preaching about hot topics: "Have you seen *Our Kind of People*, that TV drama series about Black people living on Martha's Vineyard?" "Do you think Kanye West's music career is as relevant as his latest Yeezy sneaker drop?" The bantering, jive talking, joke cracking, and loud music under a flickering candle is my juke joint, my version of the once thriving clandestine blues-and-booze establishments clustered mostly in the Deep South. Call it Taylor's juke joint, a Harlem Renaissance salon, or a makeshift meat-and-three, I've effortlessly gathered folks on my terrace in Flatbush, Brooklyn, for red drinks on Juneteenth or under the August moon on a random weekend. Making red drinks is communion, a libation to old and new sacrifices—the future and past illuminated through the glass. A sip takes you on a rapturous journey from where we've been to where we're going.

GINGER BEER

MAKES 1 GALLON

After buying glorious fresh ginger from Derek Pope and Sydney Buffington, the husband-and-wife duo behind Ladybird Farm in Hull, Georgia, I asked about the plant's beautiful ornamental-looking leaves. This was when I realized that I had never paid attention to the anatomy of ginger straight from the ground. It looks like a houseplant, but so tall it nearly touches the top of my tightly coiled hair. In earnest, developing this recipe was my return to fermenting. It felt good to truly babysit a drink for 10 days.

GINGER STARTER:

1 (1-inch) piece fresh ginger, peeled and finely grated, plus more as needed for daily feedings (7 to 10 teaspoons)

1 tablespoon sugar, plus more as needed for daily feedings (7 to 10 teaspoons)

1 cup filtered water

GINGER BEER:

1 gallon filtered water, at room temperature

1¼ cups sugar, plus more as needed

½ cup fresh lemon juice (about 3 lemons)

⅓ cup finely grated fresh ginger

FOR THE GINGER STARTER: In a sanitized quart-size glass jar, combine the ginger, sugar, and water. Cover with cheesecloth or a clean dish towel and secure with a rubber band. Place the jar in a warm, dark place out of direct sunlight for 24 hours.

After 24 hours, the starter may have small bubbles or look the same. Feed the starter by stirring in 1 teaspoon finely grated fresh ginger and 1 teaspoon sugar once a day for 7 to 10 days. When the mixture is bubbling undisturbed, it's ready to use.

FOR THE GINGER BEER: In a sanitized glass jug or other nonreactive container, combine 1 cup of the ginger starter, the water, sugar, lemon juice, and ginger. Cover with cheesecloth or a clean dish towel and secure with a rubber band. Place the jug in a warm, dark place out of direct sunlight for 8 to 10 days, stirring the ginger beer twice a day and tasting for sweetness. Add 1 tablespoon sugar maximum per day if needed. When white natural yeast appears at the bottom of the jug and the ginger beer bubbles when you stir, it's done with its first fermentation.

Transfer the ginger beer to clean bottles with tight-sealing lids. Seal the bottles and store in a dark room at room temperature (70º to 75ºF) to ferment for 2 days. If it's too warm, the ginger beer will need less time to ferment and might explode if left unattended for too long. Move the bottles to the refrigerator and consume within 3 days.

WATERMELON GINGER BEER

MAKES 4 DRINKS

You'll need the juice from a red-fleshed watermelon for this batch drink. I love the rare seeded watermelon, but they are hard to find and can be a pain if you're using a blender, as you'll need to strain the juice afterward. If you own a juicer, proceed with the seeds and all. Watermelon is over 90 percent water and is a nutrient-dense food. This drink can serve as an everyday accompaniment at breakfast, lunch, dinner, or with a snack.

2 tablespoons fresh fennel fronds (optional)

Filtered water

6 cups cubed watermelon

2 cups ginger beer, homemade (see page 55) or store-bought

Divide the fennel fronds (if using) between two ice cube trays. Fill with water and freeze until solid, 4 to 8 hours.

Meanwhile, place the watermelon in a blender or food processor and blend until smooth. Scrape the sides of the blender or food processor using a rubber spatula and blend again.

Place a metal sieve over a large bowl and strain the pureed watermelon through the sieve (this should yield about 2 cups of juice). Store in the refrigerator until ready to serve; it will keep in the fridge for about 3 days.

To serve, fill four highball glasses or rocks glasses with the fennel ice cubes. Add ½ cup of the watermelon juice to each glass and top off with the ginger beer.

TIP: Unlike ginger ale, ginger beer is fermented. The nonalcoholic drink has a spicy kick and tends to have more flavor than the soft drink version. If buying ginger beer from the store, I recommend Barritt's or Bruce Cost.

MARIGOLD GIN SOUR

MAKES 4 DRINKS

Marigold flowers marry perfectly with a botanical-forward gin cocktail. Marigold's musky yet sweet scent smells like summer. The egg gives this cocktail an appealing foam cap. Don't be afraid to embrace the raw whites. I'd recommend pouring the drink into a coupe or cosmopolitan glass after shaking; it shows off that frothy cap nicely.

MARIGOLD SYRUP (MAKES 1½ CUPS):

1 cup water

1 cup sugar

½ cup dried marigolds, or 1 cup fresh marigold petals (green centers removed)

GIN SOUR:

8 ounces gin

2 ounces marigold syrup

4 ounces fresh lemon juice

4 large egg whites (2 ounces)

Aromatic bitters

Fresh marigold petals or fresh herbs, for garnish (optional)

FOR THE MARIGOLD SYRUP: In a small saucepan, combine the water and sugar and stir to combine. Bring a boil over medium-high heat and whisk to dissolve the sugar for 1 minute. Remove from the heat and stir in the marigold petals. Transfer to a heatproof container and allow to cool to room temperature, then refrigerate for 24 hours.

Strain the marigold syrup through a fine-mesh sieve into a medium bowl, discarding the petals. Transfer the strained syrup to a squeeze bottle and refrigerate until ready to use. The syrup can be refrigerated for up to several weeks.

FOR THE COCKTAIL: In a cocktail shaker, combine 4 ounces of the gin, 2 ounces of the lemon juice, 1 ounce of the egg white, and 1 ounce of the marigold syrup. Shake without ice for 10 seconds to froth the egg white, then add ice and shake for another 10 seconds until chilled.

Strain the cocktail into two of the prepared coupes and add 2 dashes of bitters, if desired. Repeat with the remaining ingredients to make two additional cocktails.

STRAWBERRY LEMONADE

MAKES 1¼ CUPS POWDERED MIX, FOR 8 CUPS LEMONADE

For a few years, Chef Omar Tate, a Philadelphia native and founder of Honeysuckle Community Center, gifted me his homemade "Kool-Aid" for Juneteenth. Before COVID-19 shut down NYC, I witnessed Omar's ceremonial unison of water and powder made from ground dehydrated fruit. He was hosting a supper club and one of the guests was the late Quandra Prettyman, cookbook collector, professor of Black literature, and Barnard's first Black full-time faculty member. Finally, I asked him to share his recipe. If your family picks strawberries in spring, you can dehydrate and store them. Otherwise, Trader Joe's sells freeze-dried and dehydrated fruit, and the citric acid can be found online.

½ cup (12g) freeze-dried strawberries

1 cup sugar

1 tablespoon citric acid

¼ teaspoon kosher salt

1 cup fresh lemon juice (about 4 lemons), plus 3 lemons for garnish

1 cup fresh strawberries, plus more for garnish

8 cups water

Ice

Combine the freeze-dried strawberries and sugar in a mini food processor and blend until they become a fine powder. Transfer to an airtight container, add the citric acid and salt, and stir to combine. (The strawberry powder can be stored in the airtight container at room temperature for up to several weeks.)

Juice the 4 lemons and slice the remaining lemons into thin wheels. Set aside.

To make a large batch of lemonade, combine all the strawberry powder with 8 cups water and the lemon juice in a large pitcher. Stir using a wooden spoon until the powder is dissolved completely. Add more water to taste, aiming for the lemonade to be on the sweeter side (the ice will dilute it slightly). Strain the lemonade through a fine-mesh sieve, if necessary, and chill until ready to serve. To serve, add the lemon slices and fresh strawberries to the pitcher and top it off with ice.

For an individual serving of lemonade, mix 2 tablespoons of the strawberry powder, 1 cup water, and 2 tablespoons lemon juice in a tall glass. Stir with a spoon until the powder is dissolved. Add ice and garnish with lemon slices and a couple of fresh and rinsed strawberries.

TIP: A dehydrator is a convenient way to take the abundance you have when the fruit is in season and extend it into those months when fresh fruit is rare. If you wish to dry your own fruit, like the strawberries for this recipe, or grapes, or oranges, slice them into ¼-inch-thick slices and use a dehydrator to dry them according to the manufacturer's instructions, 6 to 8 hours, depending on the machine. Store the dried fruit in an airtight container, with plenty of air to breathe at the top, at room temperature for several months.

AFRO EGG CREAM

MAKES 4 DRINKS

Marguerite Hannah, 61. Born and raised in Galveston, Texas, Marguerite's voice lit up as she talked about her Juneteenth foods: brisket, hot links, stuffed shrimp, potato salad, and lemon pie. One of the most memorable moments in our phone conversation was Marguerite waxing poetic about her childhood throwbacks of red cream soda.

Later, as I read more about Black Galveston and made a pilgrimage to Galveston Island, I connected the dots that Marguerite is the granddaughter of Thomas Deboy "T.D." Armstrong, one of the most prominent businessmen in Galveston, who once graced the list of the 100 richest African Americans in the US. The Fountain Luncheonette at Armstrong's drugstore was a popular community gathering spot. Marguerite's mother worked there as a soda jerk, and served a lot of things, including hot dogs, fries, ice cream, malts, and the most talked-about menu item, cherry cola.

There was another drink popular at drugstores of the day: the egg cream. That drink, which contained no egg, was a combination of chocolate syrup, milk, and soda water. This Afro egg cream or French soda modernizes the classic by combining it with the flavors of red drink. I close my eyes and imagine sitting at the booth near Mr. Armstrong's outside marquee sign, letting the sunlight hit my face as I enjoy my red drink.

8 ounces sweetened hibiscus tea

1 ounce heavy cream

4 ounces seltzer

12-16 cubes of ice

SWEET HIBISCUS TEA:

4 cups hibiscus tea (recipe follows)

1½ cups simple syrup (page 244)

Combine the hibiscus tea and simple syrup in a small pitcher and stir. Set aside.

Fill four goblet glasses with ice, divide equally 8 ounces of sweetened tea into the glasses. Very slowly pour in the heavy cream. If your sugar quantity is off in your tea mixture or you switch out the dairy, this cream soda may curdle (the hibiscus tea is acidic). If this happens, start again and add a little more simple syrup to your glass. Otherwise, proceed with the seltzer and then stir. The mixture will be a creamsicle red. Serve.

HIBISCUS TEA

MAKES 4 CUPS

4 cups water

1 cup dried hibiscus flowers

½ teaspoon ground ginger

In a medium saucepan or kettle, bring the water to a boil over high heat. Add the hibiscus flowers and remove from the heat. Cover and let steep for 10 minutes. Stir in the ginger and let cool completely. Using a funnel and a fine-mesh strainer, discard the flowers and transfer the tea to an airtight container. Store in the refrigerator for up to 1 week.

COLOR-CODED

This hibiscus tea (minus the sweetener) is known as bissap in Senegal, where it's the national drink; in North Africa, it's karkadeh.

In the Caribbean, it's called sorrel, and in Mexico, agua de Jamaica. And at Black American gatherings and in pop culture, it's called "red drink." I'd declare any vibrant and bright beverage, soda, fruit juice, or spritz A-OK for Juneteenth, but remember to thank the descendants of enslaved Africans for keeping this ritual alive.

The hibiscus flower is native to tropical and subtropical regions, but more and more farmers in the American South are growing it. Here's what to know when you shop for it: If you're traveling to a farmers' market, you may see hibiscus flower buds. If you're shopping at a specialty store or online grocer, you'll see dried petals. Both can be steeped in water and made into red drink.

MAROON MARGARITA

MAKES 4 DRINKS

This cocktail is the official drink of our "down south" residence, the Maroon House: an ode to enslaved Blacks who escaped plantations to establish settlements in remote places like the Great Dismal Swamp in Virginia and North Carolina, and the Florida Everglades. We are sort of escaping in reverse, leaving the Northern hustle for the calm Southern sanity. A journey like that calls for its own drink!

MAROON MARGARITA MIX (MAKES 1½ CUPS):

⅓ cup unsweetened coconut flakes

¼ teaspoon kosher salt

2 cups packed dark brown sugar

1 cup water

3 cups hulled strawberries

Zest of 2 limes

Juice of 8 limes

MARGARITA:

¼ cup kosher salt, for rimming the glass

Zest of 1 orange (about 3 tablespoons)

2 limes, cut into wedges

Ice

4 ounces margarita mix

3 ounces tequila

1 ounce orange liqueur

FOR THE MAROON MARGARITA MIX: In a medium saucepan, toast the coconut flakes over medium-low heat until golden brown, 3 to 4 minutes. Add the salt, sugar, water, strawberries, and lime zest and juice. Bring to a boil, then reduce the heat to low to maintain a simmer. Partially cover the pot and simmer, stirring occasionally, for about 40 minutes, or until the liquid is thickened to a syrup. About halfway through the cooking time, begin mashing the strawberries using a potato masher and continue to mash occasionally as they cook. Remove from the heat and allow to cool completely. (The margarita mix will keep in an airtight container in the refrigerator for several weeks.)

FOR THE MARGARITA: Combine the salt and the orange zest on a plate. Run the lime wedges around the rims of four rocks glasses. Dip the rims into the orange salt to coat and set aside.

In a cocktail shaker filled with ice, combine 4 ounces of the margarita mix, the tequila, and the orange liqueur. Shake for 15 seconds, until frothy, then strain into the prepared cocktail glasses over ice. Serve.

SWEET POTATO SPRITZ

MAKES 4 DRINKS

In *Invisible Man*, the 1953 National Book Award–winning and bestselling novel by Ralph Ellison, Ellison writes vividly about his protagonist purchasing warm, round, butter-topped sweet potatoes from street cart vendors in Harlem. His description of the no-frills snack is vivid: "I knew that it was sweet before I broke it; bubbles of brown syrup had burst the skin." Reading that made my mouth water and inspired me to create this drink. Make one and start reading Ellison's second novel, *Juneteenth*, published in 1999, five years after his death.

SWEET POTATO SYRUP
(MAKES 3½ CUPS):

2 cups sugar

2½ cups water

1 sweet potato, peeled and cut into ½-inch pieces

½ vanilla bean, split lengthwise

1 star anise pod

¼ teaspoon ground cinnamon

½ teaspoon ground cardamom

¼ teaspoon kosher salt

SPRITZ:

Ice

8 ounces Aperitivo Cappelletti

3 ounces vodka

2 ounces sweet potato syrup

16 ounces sparkling wine

4 dehydrated orange slices (see Tip, page 60), for garnish

FOR THE SWEET POTATO SYRUP: Combine the sugar, water, sweet potato, vanilla bean, star anise, cinnamon, cardamom, and salt in a medium saucepan. Bring to a boil over medium-low heat, then reduce the heat to low and simmer, stirring frequently, until the sugar is dissolved and the sweet potato is tender, about 15 minutes. Remove from the heat and allow the sweet potato to steep in the syrup for 1 to 2 hours, until cooled to room temperature. Strain the syrup through a fine-mesh sieve and use the sweet potato for another recipe (it's great on toast!). (The simple syrup can be stored in an airtight container in the refrigerator for up to several weeks.)

FOR THE SPRITZ COCKTAIL: In a cocktail shaker filled with ice, combine 4 ounces of the Cappelletti, 1½ ounces of the vodka, and 2 ounces of the sweet potato syrup. Stir using a long bar spoon until combined. Strain into two large stemless or stemmed wineglasses over ice and top each with 4 ounces sparkling wine. Repeat to make two additional cocktails. Garnish each cocktail with a dried orange slice.

BLUEBERRY & BAY LEAF TONIC

MAKES 4 DRINKS

I always start every gathering at home, big or small, with a toast or head-bowed blessing. I don't really believe in those sleeves of blue or red plastic cups that are so common at large gatherings. If I've gone to the trouble of crafting a signature drink for the evening, I've also gone to the trouble of selecting ornate drinkware from which to consume it. Often I get my culinary inspiration by taking common ingredients and using them in unexpected ways. That's the philosophy behind this drink. Fresh bay leaf has such a rich, herbaceous flavor, and I store it in the fridge to preserve that. Dried bay leaves or bay laurel is a common pantry ingredient, and I make certain to use them within a month of opening the jar. Why not put it in a cocktail?

Ice

2 ounces brine from Quick-Pickled Blueberries (page 43)

4 ounces Lemon Cordial (page 72)

24 ounces tonic water

Quick-Pickled Blueberries (page 43), for garnish

4 bay leaves, for garnish

Fill four cosmo glasses with ice. Divide the brine from the pickled blueberries and the lemon cordial among the glasses. Stir to combine and top with the tonic water. Serve garnished with pickled blueberries and a bay leaf on a cocktail pick.

NOTE: A few of the quick-pickled vegetables and fruits in this book can be use in a tonic like this one. Just substitute the brine from the Quick-Pickled Blueberries for brine from Quick-Pickled Squash Spears (page 44) or Quick-Pickled Purple Carrots (page 45) and proceed as directed.

LEMON CORDIAL

MAKES 4 CUPS

Zest and juice of 10 lemons (about 2 cups juice and ½ cup zest)

3 cups sugar

2 cups water

Using a Microplane or zester, zest the lemons into a small bowl and set aside. Roll the zested lemons against the counter to release as much juice as possible, then slice in half and squeeze the juice into a separate small bowl.

In a medium saucepan, combine the sugar and water and bring to a boil over high heat. Cook, whisking continuously, until the sugar is dissolved, about 1 minute. Stir in the lemon zest and juice. Bring the mixture back to a boil, whisking once or twice. Remove from the heat and allow to cool to room temperature, 10 to 15 minutes. Strain the mixture through a fine-mesh sieve into an airtight container. Store in the refrigerator until ready to use, up to several weeks.

MISO BLOODY MARY

MAKES 4 DRINKS

I've hosted brunches where the food was reheated at five p.m. because people were still hanging out and were hungry again. And if people are ready to eat again, then they are probably ready to drink again as well. In my opinion, this shaken version of a Bloody Mary has no time designation. It's good morning, noon, or night. The classic Bloody Mary has tomato juice, vodka, and seasonings ranging from Worcestershire sauce to horseradish. I've extended that range. I knew that miso, a traditional Japanese paste most often made from fermented soybeans and rice, gives this cocktail majestic flavor. This umami bomb is accessible on many supermarket shelves, but a great substitute is good soy sauce or fish sauce.

4 ounces vodka

10 ounces tomato juice

½ teaspoon light miso paste

2 sprigs tarragon

Juice of 2 small limes (4 tablespoons)

1 teaspoon chili powder

Ice

Quick-Pickled Banana Peppers (page 44), cherry tomatoes, radishes, and Quick-Pickled Squash Spears (page 44), for garnish

In a cocktail shaker, combine the vodka, tomato juice, miso paste, tarragon, lime juice, and chili powder and muddle using a wooden spoon. Add ice to the shaker, cover, and shake for 30 seconds, until combined and chilled. Strain the mixture into four highball glasses over ice and garnish with pickled banana peppers, cherry tomatoes, radishes, and spears of pickled yellow squash.

FESTIVALS & FAIRS

FESTIVALS & FAIRS

From the beginning, the creation of "wilderness" and public lands (parks and forests) was the centerpiece to the nation-building project of defining who we are as Americans. These lands were our cathedrals, our representations to the world of, supposedly, the best of who we are and who we can be. From the beginning, African Americans as well as other nonwhite peoples were not allowed to participate on their own terms in this project. —Carolyn Finney, *Black Faces, White Spaces*

istening to the bass line and whistles in Beyoncé's "Black Parade" and OutKast's "Morris Brown" hypes me up in the same manner as watching videos of the Tuskegee University band, the Marching Crimson Pipers, with students swaying to their pep chant, "Ball and Parlay." That music gives me invincible energy, the same feeling of attending Atlanta's Sweet Auburn Festival—my first bath in the essence of an outdoor bacchanal. The sloshing of big cups of lemonade and the blaring of the MC making announcements on the main stage, long lines to get Black Bart Simpson T-shirts, fresh fried fish, funnel cakes, and nachos were a springtime rite of passage.

Spaces like parks, fairgrounds, streetways, and river walks have long been locations of leisure for Black Americans, places to gather and listen, play, and eat. The great migrations of the twentieth century, which transformed US cities, made these outdoor spaces even more important. From the beginning of the 1900s to the early 1970s, millions of African Americans left towns like Marion, Alabama, and Denmark, South Carolina, for better jobs, better education, and a chance to dodge the "in your face" discrimination they faced below the Mason-Dixon Line. These outdoor spaces were extensions of their new homes.

In 2011, I attended my first-ever Juneteenth festival in Cuyler Gore, a triangular park in Brooklyn's Fort Greene neighborhood. The festival was the eleventh annual celebration of Juneteenth organized by the CoOperative Culture Collective; vendors were selling African print dresses and horses casually trotted by with kids in the saddle. It reminded me of a tiny Texas Juneteenth fair.

The word "fair" sounds so fun and so innocent. But like many words in the American lexicon, it is drenched in racial and racist history. For a generation of Black Americans, festivals or fairs were a prideful event to showcase ingenuity in the arts and sciences and beyond, as well as a reminder of white supremacy attempting to control Black life. There's no way to better describe that juxtaposition than the Texas state fair. The fair dates back to 1886 and is held in Dallas's Fair Park. Three years after it started, the fair's organizers created "Colored People's Day," which is to say that all the other days of the fair were not for "colored people." In the early 1900s, that day was eliminated, and African Americans were outlawed from the fair until 1936. It wasn't until the 1960s that the fair was desegregated. But even before that, Black celebrities appeared at the fair: Booker T. Washington walked the grounds in 1900, and Louis Armstrong gave four concerts in one day in 1956. In more modern times, Tye Tribbett, Ne-Yo, and Tamia have alternated onstage with Black Pumas, Banda Carnaval, and La Energía Norteña.

It's more than classic American comfort food like corn dogs, turkey legs, elephant ears, and Frito pies that keeps Black Americans connected to traditions like fairs and festivals, and to places like Texas. We molded the wards of Houston and the U and H Street corridors in DC. We coalesce in backyards, melding together the places we know and the varied cultures around us, and mixing American traditions. These places wouldn't be the same without us.

FUNNEL CAKE

WITH APPLE TOPPING

MAKES 4

You can't entirely separate Juneteenth from other summer festivals and celebrations and their menus. But while funnel cakes are common at state fairs and the like, most people don't make them at home. It's really not that hard to do, once you master the art of swirling the batter in the hot oil. The delicately spiced batter makes this version a cut above your regular fairground funnel cake. Even without the fruit topping, these are delicious.

APPLE TOPPING:

1 tablespoon unsalted butter

1½ cups small-diced (¼ inch) peeled tart apples, such as Granny Smith

2 tablespoons pure maple syrup

½ teaspoon ground cinnamon

¼ teaspoon ground star anise

¼ teaspoon kosher salt

FUNNEL CAKE:

2 quarts peanut oil, for frying

1¼ cups all-purpose flour

2 tablespoons packed dark brown sugar

2 teaspoons baking powder

¼ teaspoon kosher salt

2 large eggs

1 cup whole milk

2 teaspoons vanilla extract

2 tablespoons seltzer

½ cup confectioners' sugar, for dusting

Special equipment: piston funnel

FOR THE APPLE TOPPING: In a small saucepan, melt the butter over medium heat. Add the apples, maple syrup, cinnamon, star anise, and salt and stir to combine. Cook, stirring occasionally, for 4 to 5 minutes, until the apple has softened. Remove from the heat and allow to cool until warm.

FOR THE FUNNEL CAKES: In a large Dutch oven or heavy-bottomed pot, heat the peanut oil over medium-high heat until it reaches 375ºF on an instant-read or deep-fry thermometer. Line a baking sheet with paper towels and set it nearby.

In a large bowl, whisk together the flour, brown sugar, baking powder, and salt to combine.

continued on page 84

In a separate medium bowl, whisk together the eggs, milk, and vanilla until smooth and combined. Add the seltzer and whisk again to combine.

Make a well in the dry mixture and pour the wet mixture into the center of the well. Whisk the wet mixture into the dry mixture until just combined and no lumps remain—the batter should resemble pancake batter.

The funnel cakes can be formed with a piston funnel or a squeeze bottle. If using a piston funnel, follow the gadget's instructions: Pour ½ cup of the batter into the funnel. Holding the funnel over the oil, release and swirl the batter into the oil, moving the funnel in a circular pattern and then crisscrossing the batter over itself. If using the squeeze bottle, squeeze ½ cup of the batter into the oil in a circular motion, then crisscross the batter over itself. Fry for 2 to 3 minutes, until golden brown on the bottom, then flip the cake using a spider or metal tongs and fry for 2 to 3 minutes, until golden brown on the other side. Transfer the funnel cake to the prepared baking sheet to drain and repeat until all the batter is used.

Using a mesh sieve, generously sprinkle the confectioners' sugar over the funnel cakes and serve immediately with the warm apple topping.

NOTE: Apples like Honeycrisp, Granny Smith, or Jonagold can be peeled, diced, and sautéed for the funnel cake topping. Mangoes like the Glenn variety can be used in the same manner as apple here, too.

FRY TIME

Is this your first time deep-frying? Let's have a talk. Beginners often worry about the oil temperature. I don't these days, because I follow these tips:

Use a large Dutch oven or heavy-bottom pan.

Look for your oil to reach 350ºF.

No higher than 375ºF, before you start frying. Your sweet spot for each food is listed in the recipe.

Fry in batches.

Maybe start with a small funnel cake. Maybe do one corn dog first, instead of three. Go small or go home.

Follow your instincts in terms of color.

If something turns dark, even if your thermometer is at your sweet spot, take the food out of the oil. Don't rely on just your thermometer. You know what looks burnt or undercooked and what looks delicious.

CORN DOGS

MAKES 6

The land of liberty, my native country, can't claim to have invented the hot dog, but we did invent the corn dog. Carl and Neil Fletcher were the first people to deep-fry hot dogs in cornbread batter, a concoction invented and sold as "Fletcher's CornyDogs" at the Texas state fair in 1942.

2 quarts peanut oil, for frying

6 hot dogs

2 tablespoons cornstarch

CORN DOG BATTER:

1 cup all-purpose flour

1 cup yellow cornmeal

2 teaspoons baking powder

½ teaspoon baking soda

2 teaspoons sugar

1½ teaspoons fresh thyme

½ teaspoon garlic powder

1½ teaspoons kosher salt

1 large egg

1½ cups light beer

Special equipment: 6 wooden skewers

In a large Dutch oven or heavy-bottomed pot, heat the peanut oil over medium-high heat until it reaches 375ºF on an instant-read or deep-fry thermometer. Line a plate with paper towels and set it nearby.

Insert a skewer halfway into each hot dog. Place the cornstarch in a baking dish and dust each hot dog with the cornstarch, shaking off any excess. Set aside.

FOR THE CORN DOG BATTER: In a large bowl, whisk together the flour, cornmeal, baking powder, baking soda, sugar, thyme, garlic powder, and salt until well combined. Add the egg and the beer to the dry ingredients and whisk until smooth and combined; the batter should be thicker than pancake batter, more like a thin cake batter.

Pour the batter into a tall glass and dip each hot dog into the batter to fully coat, allowing the excess to drip off. Immediately place the hot dog in the hot oil and fry until golden brown, 3 to 4 minutes. Use metal tongs to flip the corn dog over to brown the other side. When the corn dog is golden, use the tongs to grab the end of the skewer and transfer it to the paper towel–lined plate. Repeat with the remaining hot dogs. Serve immediately.

ZUCCHINI CORN DOGS

WITH CORN CREMA

MAKES 4

My sophomore year at Clark Atlanta University, I was living in Brawley Hall, in a four-room suite complete with kitchen. You could not have told me back then that preparing steamed broccoli, boiled corn on the cob, and bags of frozen vegetables wasn't serious cooking. Besides, I'd work some chicken fingers and french fries into the rotation, too. My vegetable vocabulary has expanded considerably since, though my palate still craves the nostalgic from time to time. This recipe honors the vegetables I discovered later, but uses a technique I've always loved. It's traditional fair food for the vegan crowd.

ZUCCHINI CORN DOGS:

4 tablespoons fresh lime juice (about 2 limes)

1 teaspoon red pepper flakes

1 teaspoon kosher salt

2 quarts peanut oil, for frying

4 small zucchini, stem ends trimmed

2 tablespoons cornstarch

1 recipe Corn Dog batter (see page 87)

Corn Crema (page 90)

Special equipment: 4 wooden skewers

CORN CREMA (MAKES 2 CUPS):

1 tablespoon unsalted butter

2 cups fresh corn kernels (cut from the cob)

2 cups sour cream

FOR THE ZUCCHINI CORN DOGS: In a large Dutch oven or heavy-bottomed pot, heat the peanut oil over medium-high heat until it reaches 375ºF on an instant-read or deep-fry thermometer. Line a plate with paper towels and set it nearby.

Insert a skewer halfway into each zucchini through the stem end, so the bottom of the zucchini is sticking upward. Lightly dampen the outside of each zucchini with water, shake off any excess, then dust the zucchini with the cornstarch.

Pour the corn dog batter into a tall glass or pitcher. Dip a skewered zucchini into the batter to fully coat, allowing the excess to drip off. Once nicely coated

continued on page 90

in batter, immediately place the zucchini in the hot oil and fry until golden brown, 3 to 4 minutes. Use metal tongs to flip the zucchini dog over to brown the other side. When the zucchini dog is golden, use the tongs to grab the end of the skewer and transfer it to the paper towel–lined plate. Repeat with the remaining zucchini. Serve immediately with the Corn Crema.

FOR THE CORN CREMA: In a medium skillet, melt the butter over medium-high heat. Add the corn kernels and cook, without stirring, for 3 minutes to allow the corn to char.

Transfer the charred kernels to a blender and add the sour cream, lime juice, red pepper flakes, and salt. Blend until smooth. Serve at room temperature or store in an airtight container in the refrigerator for up to 4 days.

TURNIP CORN BALLS

MAKES 4 SKEWERS

This is for the adults, but a young person might be into the spicy bite of a turnip. Japanese Hakurei turnips are the gateway turnip to always having root vegetables in your shopping rotation. Also called Tokyo turnips, they are mild in flavor and super delicious fried and dipped in the corn crema.

2 quarts peanut oil, for frying

2 or 3 bunches Hakurei turnips, greens removed

2 tablespoons cornstarch

1 recipe Corn Dog batter (see page 87)

Special equipment: 4 wooden skewers

In a large Dutch oven or heavy-bottomed pot, heat the peanut oil over medium-high heat until it reaches 375ºF on an instant-read or deep-fry thermometer. Line a plate with paper towels and set it nearby.

Skewer 4 to 5 turnips on each wooden skewer. Lightly dampen the outside of the turnips with water and shake off any excess. Dust the turnips with the cornstarch.

Pour the corn dog batter into a tall glass or pitcher and dip each skewer into the batter to fully coat, allowing the excess to drip off. Once nicely coated in batter, immediately place the turnip skewer in the hot oil and fry until golden brown, 3 to 4 minutes. Use metal tongs to flip the skewer over to brown the other side. When the turnip is golden, use the tongs to grab the end of the skewer and transfer it to the paper towel–lined plate. Repeat with the remaining turnips. Serve immediately.

BEER–BATTERED SHRIMP

MAKES 4 TO 6 SERVINGS, 36 TO 40 SHRIMP

I do envy people who live in cities like New Orleans, Wilmington, and the Juneteenth city of origin, Galveston. It's the fact that Juneteenth for them can often mean something other than BBQ. Gus Allen was an African American entrepreneur who owned a hotel, café, and several other businesses on Galveston's Church Street. The once-bustling strip of Black-owned commerce no longer exists, but the goodness of the people and food have been documented in *Lost Black Restaurants of Galveston's African American Community*, a book produced by the Galveston Historical Foundation. This recipe for a fried crunchy coated shrimp is in remembrance of Gus Allen and many more coastal seafood joints.

2 quarts peanut oil, for frying

1 pound medium shrimp, peeled (tails left on) and deveined (see Notes)

1 teaspoon kosher salt, plus more as needed

½ teaspoon freshly ground black pepper

1½ cups Fish Fry Mix (page 33)

1 cup beer, such as a lager

In a large Dutch oven or heavy-bottomed pot, heat the peanut oil over medium-high heat until it reaches 350ºF on an instant-read or deep-fry thermometer. Line a plate with paper towels and set it nearby.

Pat the shrimp very dry with paper towels and season with the salt and pepper.

Put the fry mix in a large bowl and whisk in the beer until the batter is combined and smooth. Dip a third of the shrimp into the batter, letting the excess run off, and place in the hot oil using metal tongs. Fry the shrimp for 2 to 4 minutes, flipping them halfway through, until golden brown and crispy. Use the tongs to transfer the shrimp to the paper towel–lined plate and season again with salt. Repeat with the remaining shrimp. Serve hot.

NOTES: If your shrimp aren't already peeled and deveined, here's how to do it: Using kitchen scissors, place the tip between the shrimp's shell and the top of its body, then cut all the way to the tail and stop, leaving the tail attached. Remove the shell and discard (or freeze for shrimp stock). To devein, run a paring knife along the shrimp's back to make a shallow cut. Look for the darkish-colored string and gently remove it with the tip of the knife, without tearing the shrimp.

BEER-BATTERED SHRIMP

MAKES 4 TO 6 SERVINGS, 36 TO 40 SHRIMP

I do envy people who live in cities like New Orleans, Wilmington, and the Juneteenth city of origin, Galveston. It's the fact that Juneteenth for them can often mean something other than BBQ. Gus Allen was an African American entrepreneur who owned a hotel, café, and several other businesses on Galveston's Church Street. The once-bustling strip of Black-owned commerce no longer exists, but the goodness of the people and food have been documented in *Lost Black Restaurants of Galveston's African American Community*, a book produced by the Galveston Historical Foundation. This recipe for a fried crunchy coated shrimp is in remembrance of Gus Allen and many more coastal seafood joints.

2 quarts peanut oil, for frying

1 pound medium shrimp, peeled (tails left on) and deveined (see Notes)

1 teaspoon kosher salt, plus more as needed

½ teaspoon freshly ground black pepper

1½ cups Fish Fry Mix (page 33)

1 cup beer, such as a lager

In a large Dutch oven or heavy-bottomed pot, heat the peanut oil over medium-high heat until it reaches 350ºF on an instant-read or deep-fry thermometer. Line a plate with paper towels and set it nearby.

Pat the shrimp very dry with paper towels and season with the salt and pepper.

Put the fry mix in a large bowl and whisk in the beer until the batter is combined and smooth. Dip a third of the shrimp into the batter, letting the excess run off, and place in the hot oil using metal tongs. Fry the shrimp for 2 to 4 minutes, flipping them halfway through, until golden brown and crispy. Use the tongs to transfer the shrimp to the paper towel–lined plate and season again with salt. Repeat with the remaining shrimp. Serve hot.

NOTES: If your shrimp aren't already peeled and deveined, here's how to do it: Using kitchen scissors, place the tip between the shrimp's shell and the top of its body, then cut all the way to the tail and stop, leaving the tail attached. Remove the shell and discard (or freeze for shrimp stock). To devein, run a paring knife along the shrimp's back to make a shallow cut. Look for the darkish-colored string and gently remove it with the tip of the knife, without tearing the shrimp.

TORNADO SWEET POTATOES

MAKES 4

When I was a kid, the best road trips were those summer church and social club excursions on charter buses to places like Six Flags Over Georgia, Myrtle Beach, Disney World, or the much-missed Cypress Gardens near Winter Haven, Florida. I was the youngest of the cousins, and my aunt would give each of us a small amount of money to spend on frozen lemonades, funnel cakes—and spiral fries. These sweet potatoes are spiraled, so there is plenty of surface area to get browned and crunchy. They'll take you as close as you're going to get to the Cypress Gardens of my youth—the amusement park is now a Legoland.

2 quarts peanut oil, for frying

4 small sweet potatoes, peeled

2 tablespoons cornstarch

Sweet Potato Seasoning (page 28)

Special equipment: potato spiral cutter, 4 wooden skewers

In a large Dutch oven or heavy-bottomed pot, heat the peanut oil over medium-high heat until it reaches 350°F on an instant-read or deep-fry thermometer. Line a plate with paper towels and set it nearby.

Using a potato spiral cutter, spiral each potato according to the manufacturer's instructions and thread the potato spiral onto a skewer. Dust the sweet potatoes with the cornstarch, shaking off any excess. Carefully separate the layers of the sweet potato on the skewer, leaving an inch at the top and bottom to act as a handle.

Place the sweet potatoes in the hot oil, one or two at a time, and fry for 3 to 4 minutes per side, until golden brown. Use metal tongs to grab the end of the skewers, transfer to the paper towel–lined plate, and immediately sprinkle with the seasoning. Repeat with the remaining sweet potatoes and serve hot.

SAVORY ELEPHANT EARS

MAKES 4 EARS

Fry bread is common among many Native American tribes, though folks don't always agree on the exact ingredients. Fry bread's cousin also owes some inspiration to another beloved dish, buñuelos, a fried bread imported from the Sephardic Jews of Spain and cemented in the various corners of the American hemisphere south of the US border. Both fry bread and buñuelos were treats I encountered trying to find something similar to the sweet elephant ears found at carnival fair food booths.

WHITE CHEDDAR POWDER:

1 cup coarsely grated white cheddar cheese

½ teaspoon cornstarch

1 teaspoon kosher salt

1 teaspoon freshly ground black pepper

ELEPHANT EARS:

1½ cups whole milk

1 tablespoon sugar

½ cup (1 stick) unsalted butter, cubed

2 tablespoons active dry yeast

4 cups all-purpose flour, plus more for dusting

2 teaspoons baking powder

1 teaspoon kosher salt

4 cups peanut oil, for frying, plus more for greasing

FOR THE WHITE CHEDDAR POWDER: Preheat the oven to its lowest setting (170ºF, if possible). Line a baking sheet with a silicone baking mat (such as a Silpat).

Evenly spread the grated cheese over the prepared baking sheet. Bake for 4 to 6 hours, until the cheese has hardened and melted into one large cracker. Halfway through the baking time, wipe any excess oil from the cheese and carefully flip it over using a large metal spatula. When the cheese has finished baking, wipe off any remaining oil and allow the cheese to cool completely, 1 to 2 hours.

continued on page 99

Savory Elephant Ears, *continued*

Crack the cooled cheese into small pieces, then, working in batches, grind the pieces in a spice grinder until a fine powder forms. Transfer the cheese powder to a small bowl, add the cornstarch, salt, and pepper, and whisk to combine. (The cheese powder can be stored in an airtight container at room temperature for up to 1 week.)

FOR THE ELEPHANT EARS: In a small saucepan, combine the milk, sugar, and 4 tablespoons of butter and heat over medium heat until the butter is melted and the sugar is just dissolved, 3 to 4 minutes. Remove the saucepan from the heat and allow the milk mixture to cool until it reaches 110ºF on an instant-read or deep-fry thermometer.

At this point, transfer the milk mixture to a large bowl and sprinkle over the yeast. Allow the yeast to bloom for 10 minutes; it should produce small bubbles, foam, and have a light scent.

Add the flour, baking powder, and salt to the yeast mixture and stir using a wooden spoon until the dough begins to come together. Transfer the dough to a floured surface and use your hands to knead until smooth and elastic, 5 to 7 minutes. Grease a large clean bowl with 1 tablespoon peanut oil to prevent the dough from sticking and place the dough in the bowl. Cover the bowl with plastic wrap, place in a warm, draft-free area, and allow to rise for 1 hour, until almost doubled in size.

Meanwhile, heat the peanut oil in a large Dutch oven or heavy-bottomed pot over medium-high heat until it reaches 375ºF on an instant-read or deep-fry thermometer. Line a baking sheet with paper towels and set it nearby.

In a small saucepan, melt the remaining 4 tablespoons of butter; set aside.

Punch the dough down after rising. Divide the dough into 4 balls and roll each ball into a ¼-inch-thick disc. Place the discs into the hot oil one at a time and fry for 1 to 2 minutes per side, flipping halfway through, until golden brown and puffed. Use metal tongs to transfer the elephant ear to the prepared baking sheet to drain. Brush the golden elephant ear with melted butter, sprinkle up to 1 tablespoon white cheddar powder over the top, and serve immediately. Repeat with the remaining dough.

NOTE: If you don't want to make cheese powder from scratch, use 1 cup store-bought white cheddar powder, or sprinkle with 1 cup nutritional yeast.

CHORIZO—CORN CHIP NACHOS

SERVES 4

In *On Juneteenth*, Annette Gordon-Reed positions the Juneteenth holiday and, from that, moves on to chronicle her upbringing in East Texas and the broader history of Texas. The moments around food were what set my drool alarm off. Gordon-Reed remembers her grandmother making hot tamales on Juneteenth—fare for a crowd. "Softening the corn husks in hot water, grinding the pork, beef, or chicken, preparing the masa dough to be spread on the husks, filling the dough with the seasoned meats, and tying the tamales for final preparation—was time-consuming. This ritual was fitting, and so very Texan," she writes. "People of African descent, and to be honest, of some European descent, celebrating the end of slavery in Texas with dishes learned in slavery and a dish favored by ancient Mesoamerican Indians that connected Texas to its Mexican past, so much Texas history brought together for this one special day." While Gordon-Reed's Juneteenth menu hearkens back nostalgically, my take on "fare for a crowd" is decidedly modern. The corn element here is not the masa in tamales or the traditional tortillas of the Mexican or Texan table. Rather, I'm using the Fritos corn chips I grew up on for my update to the classic nachos and dip.

QUESO (MAKES 2 CUPS):

8 ounces Monterey Jack cheese, grated

1 tablespoon cornstarch

1¼ cups evaporated milk

1 tablespoon hot sauce, NAT's Red Hot Sauce (page 38) or Salsa Verde (page 39)

1 teaspoon ground cumin

½ teaspoon kosher salt

NACHOS:

2 (18.5-ounce) bags corn chips, like Fritos Scoops

2 fresh Mexican chorizo sausages (10 ounces total), casings removed

½ medium white onion, diced

2 garlic cloves, minced

2 tablespoons plain full-fat yogurt

1½ cups Salsa Verde (page 39)

½ cup Quick-Pickled Purple Carrots (page 45)

2 tablespoons picked fresh cilantro leaves with a little bit of stem

continued on page 102

Chorizo-Corn Chip Nachos, *continued*

FOR THE QUESO: In a large bowl, toss the cheese and cornstarch together and set aside. In a large saucepan, heat the evaporated milk over medium heat to warm through.

Working with one handful at a time, sprinkle the cheese over the evaporated milk and whisk continuously until the cheese is melted. Continue until all the cheese is melted into the milk and the mixture is very smooth.

Add the hot sauce, cumin, and salt and whisk to combine. Cook, whisking continuously, until the mixture thickens and nicely coats the back of a spoon. Keep the queso warm over low heat and stir occasionally until ready to use. If the queso becomes too dry, just add more evaporated milk and whisk until smooth and combined.

FOR THE NACHOS: Place half the corn chips on a large platter and set aside.

In a medium saucepan, cook the chorizo over medium-high heat, breaking it up into pieces using a wooden spoon as it cooks, for 2 to 3 minutes, until some oil is released. Add half the onion and all the garlic and cook for another 3 to 5 minutes, until the onion is softened and the chorizo is browned and cooked through.

Layer half the warm queso over the corn chips and top with half the chorizo mixture. Pile the remaining corn chips on top, then top with the remaining queso and chorizo mixture. Top with the yogurt, salsa verde, pickled carrots, and cilantro. Serve hot.

WAVY FRIES

WITH BLUE CHEESE DIP & LEMON PEPPER

SERVES 4

Crinkle or wavy fries are especially golden brown and delicious because they have more nooks to socialize with the hot grease than other fries do. This means they take on more flavor. Knowing this, I wondered how to take these fries to the next level of french fry heaven. My sense memory took me back to lemon pepper wings at Atlanta's American Deli. That's it! French fries with all the cheesy goodness of a blue cheese dipping sauce and the zing of lemon pepper wings.

FRIES:

2 quarts peanut oil, for frying

4 large Idaho potatoes, peeled

½ cup crumbled blue cheese

½ cup Lemon Pepper Seasoning (page 28)

2 tablespoons chopped fresh parsley, for garnish

BLUE CHEESE DIP:

1 cup heavy cream

½ cup cornstarch

Special equipment: crinkle fry potato cutter

FOR THE FRIES: In a large Dutch oven or heavy-bottomed pot, heat the peanut oil over medium-high heat until it reaches 350ºF on an instant-read or deep-fry thermometer. Line two baking sheets with paper towels and set them nearby.

Fill a large bowl with ice and water and set it near your cutting board. With a crinkle cutter, slice the potatoes into ½-inch-long planks. Cut each plank into ½-inch-wide batons, placing the potatoes in the ice water as you finish.

FOR THE BLUE CHEESE DIP: Meanwhile, in a medium bowl, whisk together the blue cheese and cream. Set aside; the sauce will thicken as it stands.

Drain the potatoes in a colander and pat very dry with paper towels. Working in batches, toss the potatoes in the cornstarch, shaking to discard any excess, then fry in the hot oil for 8 to 10 minutes, until golden brown. Using a spider, transfer the fries to the prepared baking sheets to drain and immediately season with the lemon pepper seasoning. Serve the fries garnished with the parsley, with the blue cheese dipping sauce alongside.

RODEO TURKEY LEGS

MAKES 4 TURKEY LEGS

Our ancestors would have been shocked at the idea that you could walk into a store and buy just the legs of a turkey—and that you could get more than two of them at a time. The Turkey Parts Industrial Complex makes it easy to buy just what you want of the big bird and nothing else. The beauty-conscious might clamor to the simple salt-and-pepper-seasoned breasts, but for people craving flavor, legs are the way to go.

Brining helps ensure that the turkey legs are well seasoned all the way to the bone. The brine will soften the tendons, and the salt starts to absorb through the big bone, which also helps the legs cook faster once they hit the oven.

TURKEY AND BRINE:

6 cups hot water

½ cup kosher salt

½ cup packed light brown sugar

4 turkey legs (4 to 5 pounds total)

1 tablespoon whole black peppercorns

1 teaspoon liquid smoke

2 bay leaves

1 teaspoon Chicken Salt (page 29)

1 teaspoon garlic powder

1 teaspoon chili powder

1 teaspoon Worcestershire sauce

1 tablespoon "everyday" olive oil

2 teaspoons honey

1 teaspoon soy sauce

1 cup chicken broth, plus more if needed

FOR THE TURKEY AND BRINE: In a large stockpot or heat-safe container, combine the hot water, salt, and brown sugar and stir until the salt and sugar have dissolved.

Add a cup of ice to cool the mixture down. Place the turkey legs in the container and add the peppercorns, liquid smoke, and bay leaves. Add enough ice to cover and submerge the turkey legs. Cover and refrigerate for at least 4 hours or up to overnight to brine.

continued on page 106

Rodeo Turkey Legs, *continued*

When ready to cook, preheat the oven to 350°F. Remove the turkey legs from the brine and pat them dry.

Combine the seasoned salt, garlic powder, and chili powder in a small bowl. Rub the turkey legs with half the seasoning. In another small bowl, mix the other half of the seasoning with the Worcestershire sauce, olive oil, honey, and soy sauce and set the sauce aside.

Pour the broth into a baking sheet or large baking dish and place on the bottom rack of the oven.

Place a rack inside a roasting pan and place the turkey legs on the rack. Roast the turkey legs on the middle rack, above the broth, for 30 to 45 minutes, until they reach an internal temperature of 160°F. Turn the legs over halfway through cooking. Avoid opening the oven repeatedly. Remove the broth pan if it evaporates completely. Pour off any turkey cooking liquid into the bowl with the sauce and stir to combine. (If the juices have all evaporated, you can use ¼ cup broth in the sauce instead.)

Begin brushing the legs with the sauce using a heat-resistant brush every 10 minutes, until the skin crisps and browns nicely. Flip and repeat the basting until the legs reach an internal temperature of at least 180°F. Remove from the oven and let the legs rest for 5 minutes before serving.

COOKOUT
& BBQ

COOKOUT & BBQ

The cookout is sacred. It's the closest thing we get in modern life to the tribe gathering around the ceremonial fire. It's all the generations, all together, trying to negotiate some middle ground between the old folks' traditions and the young people's insistence on being themselves, even if the old folks don't approve.

hen I asked family to describe the quintessential Black cookout and BBQ, each gave me phrases to describe the elements of the day. Almost like a checklist. So the cookout is where the young cousin sporting her box braids introduces her new boyfriend for the first time. She seems oblivious to the fact that everyone disapproves of his gold fronts. For that matter, they are side-eyeing the shortness of her snow-white jumper. Truth be told, she's not all that happy, either—the smoke from the BBQ pit is not quite strong enough to mask the smell of the cheap cognac the drunk next-door neighbor spills from his flask as he springs up to give a fist bump. Big mamas, the eldest generation, are fixed inside the house on the living room sofa; box fans are hitting the tail end of their floral print caftans. Aunties, the second-eldest generation, are putting the final fixings on all the vegetables and sides, waiting for the meat to be ready to be put on the buffet. The young kids are either running around playing, oblivious to everything, or constantly asking when the food will be ready. I have been a member of those two younger generations. I'm almost, now, of the auntie generation. Or maybe not quite.

In 2012, I held a Juneteenth picnic in Brooklyn's Prospect Park, and it felt different from celebrations organized by family. When I hosted my friends on that occasion, it wasn't in the backyard, but in a shady green patch across from the Lefferts Historic House Museum. According to the 1800 census, twelve enslaved Black people were forced to provide free labor inside that eighteenth-century house. That fact was in the background as we poured cocktails, listened to music,

smelled the wildflowers bought from BK Farmyards, and noshed on oven-roasted pork shoulder, potato salad, pickled vegetables, cornbread, and a strawberry crisp. The food was good; the company was better; the spirit of the Black cookout continued.

Some recipes in this chapter are for pulling out a kettle grill for chicken burgers and smoked sausages, because a Juneteenth celebration is always a cookout and often a barbecue. Others, like the Caraway Butter Trout, beef ribs, and pork chops, are for the barbecue; you see the smoke, you need the smoke.

Gather your tribe whenever you can. Feed them well.

MEATLESS BAKED BEANS

SERVES 6 TO 8

I know the words "vegan and vegetarian" scare people off, especially on a holiday, but I promise you, this dish goes well with all mains. It's also fine by itself. The key to this is the texture of the mushrooms. I advise you to splurge on the shiitake variety here; they are more expensive than button, but the texture has a feeling of not-yet-crispy bacon that you'll like, and the flavor has a subtle smokiness that you'll want. If you like, you can use a food processor instead of chopping the fungi by hand. Roll with canned beans in a time crunch (drain and rinse them and proceed with the recipe).

2 cups dried navy beans, or 6 cups cooked or canned navy beans, drained and rinsed

4 cups vegetable stock (if using canned beans, use 2 cups)

2 tablespoons "everyday" olive oil

1 cup chopped yellow onion

1 cup chopped green bell pepper

2 garlic cloves, minced

1½ cups minced stemmed shiitake mushrooms

1 tablespoon tomato paste

2 cups Rhubarb BBQ Sauce (page 35)

1 teaspoon smoked paprika

1 teaspoon kosher salt

1 teaspoon freshly ground black pepper

If using dried beans, sort through them and pick out any debris. Place the beans in a large bowl and cover with 8 cups of water. Set aside to soak for at least 2 hours or up to overnight.

Drain the beans in a colander, discarding the liquid, and transfer to a large Dutch oven or heavy-bottomed pot. Add the stock and bring it to a boil over high heat, then reduce the heat to maintain a simmer. Simmer for 1 hour, or until the beans are tender but not mushy. Remove from the heat.

If using canned beans, combine the beans and 2 cups of stock in a large Dutch oven or heavy-bottomed pot and warm over medium heat for 10 to 15 minutes.

Preheat the oven to 375°F.

In a separate large Dutch oven or heavy-bottomed pot, heat the olive oil over medium heat. Add the onion and cook for about 2 minutes, or until softened. Add the bell pepper, garlic, and mushrooms and cook, stirring occasionally, for 6 to 8 minutes, until fragrant and the mushrooms are beginning to brown.

Push all the vegetables to the side of the pot, add the tomato paste, and cook for a minute to caramelize. Add the BBQ sauce and stir to combine until smooth. Increase the heat to high and bring the sauce to a boil, then add the beans with the stock, paprika, salt, and black pepper. (You can make the baked beans a day in advance and place in the fridge here.)

Place the Dutch oven or pot in the oven and bake, uncovered, for about 45 minutes, or until the sauce is thick and bubbling. Allow to cool for 30 minutes before serving.

NOTE: The other option here is the grill: Heat a grill to low (250°F). Place the bean mixture in a medium to large aluminum pan. Place on the not-so-hot spot of the grill, close the lid, and cook for 1 hour 30 minutes.

WHO GRILLIN'?

Let me be honest here. My husband mans the grill and I micromanage the entire grilling process. Here are all the things you need to know to start your charcoal grill*:

What kind of grill are you using?

Pick your machinery.

Are you far away from the house?

Are you near any flammable objects? Do you have everything that you need to cook beside you, to your right or your left? Be safe as you go.

Choose your burning agent.

Coals are classic; wood chips will give food a kiss of smoke. Lighter fluid is not necessary. Forget what you heard—you do not need lighter fluid. What you do need is a chimney starter, tinder, and matches to start the fire. The coals inside the starter need to be red hot. When the fire in the starter has gone down, evenly disperse the red-hot coals on top of the unlit coals inside the grill.

Watch your flame; when the coals turn slightly ashy, it's time to drop your grate. If you're a newbie, a probe thermometer will help you know when the temperature is right. You may need to add more charcoal to get to the right grill temperature for your food.

Follow the recipe to cook your food to the desired doneness.

And when you're through, make sure your fire is completely out before you pack up.

*Make sure you clean your grates and buy the proper tools to do it.

PORK CHOPS

WITH DUKKAH

SERVES 4

The thick porterhouse style has become my go-to cut for the pork chop, but any 1-inch-thick piece like a rib chop or loin chop with the bone in will work. Brining is a game changer that gives a silky texture and a more complex taste to these pork chops, especially when you cook them to medium as recommended here. You can opt out of the dukkah and roll with grilled pork chops with any of the sauces for proteins on pages 33–40.

2 cups water

¼ cup kosher salt

2 garlic cloves, smashed and peeled

1 teaspoon whole black peppercorn

1 bay leaf

2 cups ice

4 bone-in center-cut pork chops, about 1-inch thick

1 cup Dukkah (page 32)

2 tablespoons fresh thyme leaves, for garnish

In a medium saucepan, bring the water to a boil over medium-high heat. Add the salt and stir until it is dissolved and the water is clear. Pour the hot salted water into a baking dish or heatproof container and add the garlic, peppercorns, bay leaf, and ice. Stir until the ice is melted.

Lay the pork chops in the liquid in a single layer and refrigerate for at least 4 hours or up to overnight to brine.

When ready to cook, heat a grill to medium-high (400ºF). Remove the pork chops from the brine and pat very dry with paper towels.

Place the pork chops on the hot grill and grill for 6 to 8 minutes per side, until they reach an internal temperature of 145ºF on an instant-read thermometer. Transfer the pork chops to a plate and coat generously with the dukkah. Allow to rest for 2 minutes before slicing. Serve garnished with the fresh thyme leaves.

CARAWAY BUTTER TROUT

SERVES 4

Caraway seeds, like their cousins, fennel seeds, have a subtle anise flavor. They play a supporting role in flavoring rye bread and sauerkraut. But here the dried fruit of the caraway plant are a bit more prominent in flavoring trout—and the result is even bigger when lemon juice is added. If you can, grill the fish on cedar planks. Nothing else gives quite the same flavor.

½ cup (1 stick) unsalted butter, at room temperature

1 tablespoon caraway seeds

zest of 1 lemon

2 tablespoons fresh lemon juice (about 2 lemons)

4 whole trout (about 2 pounds of fish total), cleaned and scaled

1 tablespoon "everyday" olive oil

1 tablespoon sea salt

1 bunch scallions

Special equipment: grill fish basket or cedar planks

If using cedar planks, soak them in water for at least 1 hour before grilling.

FOR THE CARAWAY BUTTER: In a small bowl, combine the butter, caraway seeds, and lemon zest and juice and stir using a spoon until smooth. Place the butter mixture on a sheet of parchment or waxed paper and form it into a log. Roll the butter log up in the parchment and twist the sides to seal. Freeze the butter for 1 hour or chill in the refrigerator for 3 hours, until solid and easy to slice.

FOR THE TROUT: When ready to cook the trout, remove the fish from the refrigerator at least 15 to 30 minutes before grilling. Heat a charcoal or gas grill to medium-high (400ºF).

continued on page 120

Caraway Butter Trout, *continued*

Slice the butter log into ½-inch-thick rounds. Place them on a parchment-lined plate and keep in a cool place, like the refrigerator, while cooking the trout.

Pat the fish very dry with paper towels. Rub the fish on both sides with the olive oil and season with the salt. Place the fish in a single layer in a nonstick grill basket and lock the basket, being sure to leave a little bit of space between each fish. (This may need to be done in batches, depending on the size of your grill basket.) If you prefer to use a cedar plank, lay the scallions down on the plank and place the fish on top.

Place the fish and scallions over indirect heat and close the grill lid. If using a grill basket, cook the fish for 6 to 8 minutes on each side and the scallions for 2 minutes on each side, until the fish is cooked to 145ºF; it should be opaque in color, easy to flake with the prongs of a fork, and lightly charred on the outside.

Immediately transfer the hot fish to a serving platter and place the charred scallions on top. Top with a few rounds of the caraway butter. Let rest for 5 minutes, then serve, spooning the melted butter back onto the fish.

PEACH & MOLASSES CHICKEN

SERVES 6 TO 8

In my local supermarket, I'm hard-pressed to find chicken thighs with the skin on. Skinless thighs have become the default variety. But so much of the fat and flavor comes from the chicken skin that removing that outer layer is tantamount to robbing the meat of most of its taste. The crispy, charred chicken edges, drenched with sauce, only happen with skin attached. So do what it takes to find skin-on thighs.

3 to 4 pounds bone-in, skin-on chicken thighs

1½ teaspoons kosher salt

½ teaspoon freshly ground black pepper

1½ tablespoons peanut oil

1 cup Peach & Molasses Sauce (page 36)

1 tablespoon coriander seeds, crushed

Heat a grill to medium (350ºF). Pat the chicken thighs very dry with paper towels. Season on both sides with the salt and pepper. Coat with the peanut oil.

Place the chicken thighs on the hot grill, skin-side down, close the grill lid, and cook, away from any flare-ups, about 8 minutes, or until the skin lifts easily from the grill grates. Flip the chicken thighs and use a heat-resistant brush to coat with some of the sauce. Cover the grill again and cook for another 8 minutes, then flip and baste with the sauce again. Grill with the lid open for about another 10 minutes, or until the thighs reach an internal temperature of 165ºF on an instant-read thermometer. Flip the chicken skin-side up one last time and rest on an upper rack or cool side of the grill for 10 minutes, brushing on more sauce as it cooks.

Transfer the chicken to a platter and sprinkle the top with the crushed coriander, then serve.

PEPPERCORN RIB EYE

SERVES 4

Steak on the grill is classically American, but not because the average American eats steak that often. Just the opposite. For generations, steak has meant success and celebration and arrival. Eating steak is American because it represents the achievement of the American dream of prosperity. The rib eye cut is a great steak for a celebratory occasion because it's big enough to share.

4 (2-pound) bone-in rib eye steaks

4 tablespoons "everyday" olive oil

½ cup Peppercorn Rub (page 30)

Flaky sea salt, for garnish

Let the steaks come to room temperature for at least 30 minutes before grilling. Heat a charcoal or gas grill to high (450ºF). Create a hot zone by piling all the coals to one side, if using a charcoal grill, or leaving one side of the gas grill on low or no heat.

Pat the steaks very dry with paper towels. Rub each steak with 1 tablespoon of the olive oil and press the peppercorn rub into both sides, using 2 tablespoons of the rub per steak.

Sear the steaks over the coals for 3 to 5 minutes on each side, until grill marks appear.

Move the steaks to the warm part of the grill, away from the hot coals or hot zone. Close the lid and cook the steaks until they reach an internal temperature of 135ºF for medium-rare.

Transfer to a platter and let rest for 5 to 10 minutes before slicing the meat off the bone, against the grain. Garnish with flaky salt and serve.

GRILLED OYSTERS

I know, already. Juneteenth does not take place in a month with an *r*, so you're not supposed to eat oysters (I learned this tidbit from a native New Orleanian). That can be good advice when applied to raw oysters. Summer oysters sometimes carry vibrio bacteria, a pathogen that is less common in colder waters and colder months. But getting rid of vibrio, even in the summer, is pretty easy: you just have to cook the oyster. Oysters grilled on the half shell bring together the best of many worlds. They are finger food, cooked on the grill, and ready to eat in a fraction of the time it takes to cook ribs.

Buy 2 dozen oysters (ask your fishmonger for a recommendation).

Heat your grill to high (450ºF).

Remove the oysters from the fridge and scrub off any debris. Wearing cut-proof gloves (if it's your first time opening oysters), or protecting your oyster-holding hand with a thick dish towel, hold an oyster flat in your hand, find the hinge, and wedge a shucking knife in. Twist and lift the top shell upward. Cut the oyster from the shell and remove the top shell. Slice the oyster open to ensure an easy slurp.

Take a page from *New York Times* food critic Tejal Rao—she "crumples a sheet of aluminum so its grooves can support the open oysters." Using long-handled tongs, place the shucked oysters, still in their bottom shells, on the grill grates, wavy side down. If you like, top each oyster with ¼ teaspoon caraway butter (see page 118).

Close the lid and grill for 3 minutes. The goal is to keep the beautiful oyster juice in the shell. The oyster shells will darken but shouldn't be burned.

Using the tongs, remove the oysters from the grill and dress with a dash or two of NAT's Red Hot Sauce (page 38), then serve.

LATE-NIGHT STEAK TOSTADA

SERVES 8

At a cookout or BBQ, I always put aside one steak for tostadas. It is the perfect snack to coat your stomach for the last batch of spiked red drink. You can use store-bought tostada shells here or make your own. I use a homemade harissa here and it can easily be switched out for any hot sauce. The fresh corn has a nice pop of sweetness. If you are not a cilantro fan, use basil.

1 cup peanut oil

8 corn tortillas, street taco size (4½ inch)

Kosher salt

1 cup feta

1 cup iceberg lettuce, shredded

½ cup fresh sweet corn kernels (from a whole cob)

1 medium tomato, diced

1 pound Peppercorn Rib Eye (page 123), thinly sliced

Harissa (page 40), sour cream, and fresh cilantro, for serving (optional)

In a medium skillet, heat the oil over medium-high heat until it reaches around 350ºF on an instant-read or deep-fry thermometer. Line a plate with paper towels and set it nearby. Place a tortilla in the hot oil, and fry for about 2 minutes per side, until golden brown. Use metal tongs to transfer the tostada shell to the prepared plate to drain. Sprinkle salt over the top. Repeat with remaining tortillas.

Evenly distribute the cheese over each tostada shell. Then layer with the lettuce, corn, tomato, and sliced steak. Harissa, sour cream, cilantro: these next few toppings are optional, so choose what you have on hand and what you like best. Serve immediately.

VERY GREEN COLESLAW

WITH GRILLED PEPPERS

SERVES 8

Either you hate coleslaw, or it's a must for your cookout plate. I fall somewhere in the middle and view it as a condiment: it makes sauce-drenched pork taste even better, balancing out any spice. It's the grilled poblanos that make the difference for me in this dish. It does wonders for my BBQ staple.

3 poblano peppers

12 cups grated or thinly sliced green cabbage, about 2 large heads

1 cup thinly sliced scallions

1 cup seasoned rice vinegar

¼ cup sugar

¼ teaspoon salt

VERY GREEN COLESLAW DRESSING:

2 garlic cloves

¼ cup olive oil

¼ cup vinegar

½ teaspoon celery seed

¼ teaspoon salt

½ teaspoon NAT's Red Hot Sauce (page 38, optional)

Heat a charcoal or gas grill to medium-high (400ºF). Place the peppers on the hot grill over direct heat. Cook until the skin is charred, 12 to 15 minutes, turning once or twice. Transfer to a cutting board and let cool, then finely chop. (The peppers can be grilled ahead. Store in an airtight container in the refrigerator until ready to use, up to 1 day.)

In a large bowl, combine the cabbage (discarding the tough white core), scallions, vinegar, sugar, and salt. This process breaks down the cabbage and produces liquid. Feel free to pour off excess liquid before adding dressing. Add the dressing and toss until well combined and serve, or transfer to an airtight container and refrigerate until ready to serve, up to 1 to 2 days.

NOTE: If you make this in advance, it will produce more liquid. You'll need to pour it off. Your cabbage should be tender with a crunch.

DRESSING A HOT LINK

When my mama began a long rant about McEver's hot links, my California-born food writer friend Osayi Endolyn was partly amazed and partly confused. Who is Ms. McEver? And how did she inspire such a passionate rant?

Hailing from the West Coast, Osayi knew all about hot links, but knew nothing about the name brand behind our regional version of the popular sausage. Just about every big or small city grocery store, and every store in a Black neighborhood, has these stout, bright-red, pork-and-beef-mix sausage links colored with red dye. McEver's Red Hots in Georgia are one of several varieties of regional sausages found around the country. They are an essential part of Juneteenth celebrations.

In Texas the sausages vary by region. In East Texas, the beef links are called hot guts, grease balls, or juicy links. Perfected by Black pitmasters, finely ground beef is stuffed into a beet casing with lots of fats and spices, and smoked on a grill. Make your condiment choices after you throw them on the grill and char. Slather on the mustard, top it with coleslaw, or place the link on a piece of white bread, though many prefer to leave them be, too.

APRICOT LAMB CHOPS

WITH GREEN GARLIC CHIMICHURRI

SERVES 4 TO 6

I'm a Southern woman, born into a working-class family when crisp white churchgoing gloves and Sunday beer bootleggers (my hometown didn't have alcohol sales until 2012) were in serious fashion and full deep freezers were a status symbol. Lamb chops were a splurge, and slightly out of reach compared to the beef, pork, catfish, and chicken that was usually in the freezer. The sweetness of the fresh apricots plays well with the fattiness of the lamb, and teams up with the spices in the chimichurri here for a great combination. If you have a tight shopping budget, purchase lamb loins.

2 pounds bone-in lamb chops (about 8)

1 pound ripe apricots, halved and pitted

1 teaspoon kosher salt

1 teaspoon freshly ground black pepper

½ cup Green Garlic Chimichurri (page 42), plus more for serving

2 tablespoons "everyday" olive oil

Season the lamb chops and apricots with the salt and pepper on all sides and place them in a large bowl or baking dish. Add the chimichurri. Cover and let marinate in the refrigerator for at least 2 hours or up to 8 hours. In a bowl, drizzle the olive oil over the halved and pitted stone fruit and set aside.

When ready to cook, remove the lamb chops from the refrigerator and allow to come to room temperature for at least 30 minutes. Heat a charcoal or gas grill to medium-high (about 400ºF).

Grill the apricots cut-side down for 4 to 5 minutes, until charred, then flip and grill for 3 minutes to char the other side. Transfer to a large platter.

Remove the lamb chops from the marinade and place over direct heat. Grill for 3 to 5 minutes per side, until they reach an internal temperature of 130ºF on an instant-read thermometer for medium doneness. Avoid flare-ups and move the chops off the direct heat if needed, but avoid flipping the chops more than once. Transfer the lamb chops to the platter with the apricots and allow to rest for 5 minutes before serving.

Smother each lamb chop with additional chimichurri and serve.

BEEF RIBS

WITH HARISSA

SERVES 4 TO 6

There are only a handful of BBQ cookbooks by Black pitmasters published by major publishing houses. Looking at those numbers, you'd be left with the impression that African Americans have not been the heart and soul of BBQ for decades; as many Black pitmasters retired, they were not being replaced by young Black pitmasters. That seems to be changing, thankfully. BBQ is returning to its roots. People argue about whether those roots spring from Texas or Carolina, beef country or pork. This recipe works well with either meat.

4 to 5 pounds center-cut beef ribs

1 tablespoon prepared horseradish

6 tablespoons kosher salt

2 tablespoons freshly ground black pepper

1 cup Harissa (page 40)

Special equipment: 8 cups hickory wood chips

Place the wood chips in a bucket and cover with cold water. Allow to soak overnight.

Using a small knife, lift and remove the thin white membrane on the bone side of the rib rack. Rub the ribs with the horseradish, salt, and pepper. (This can be done up to a day ahead; store the ribs in a reusable storage bag.)

When you're ready to cook the ribs, heat a charcoal grill to medium-low (250ºF). Drain the wood chips and scatter a handful over the coals. Cover and wait until the wood chips start to smoke.

Place the ribs bone-side down on the cold side of the grill with the vents open. Cover and smoke the beef ribs over indirect heat until they reach an internal temperature of 250ºF on an instant-read thermometer, 5 to 6 hours. Check the temperature of the grill periodically to ensure it remains between 250º and 275ºF and move the ribs away from any hot spots or flare-ups. Add a handful of wood chips whenever the smoke dies down. After the first 3 hours, brush the harissa sauce over the meat using a heat-resistant brush, then continue basting the meat with the sauce every 20 minutes. Once fully cooked, the ribs should be tender, with the meat falling off the bone. Transfer the ribs to a baking sheet and cover lightly with foil. Allow to rest for 30 minutes before slicing.

Finish with more harissa, if desired, and serve.

WATERMELON KEBABS

WITH CITRUS VERBENA SALT

SERVES 8

Watermelons stood out in minstrel-era caricatures featuring Black people—stealing watermelons or eating watermelon and dancing or eating watermelon and doing anything that would exemplify the stereotype of the "watermelon-eating darky." It was this one-sided nineteenth- and twentieth-century white supremacist depiction of Black life that made my recipe for grilled watermelon that appeared as part of an eleven-page feature in *Food & Wine* magazine uncomfortable for some Black Americans. I was proud of the recipe and happy that my personal stories of celebrating Juneteenth had appeared in a print magazine. But then the Shade Room, a Black entertainment gossip website, in its rush to throw shade, drew the worst conclusion: that I was in fact "dancing," or merely entertaining non-Black readers. My unwavering commitment to telling our stories of Black celebrations can't be canceled.

1 large seedless watermelon

4 teaspoons Citrus Verbena Salt (page 30)

2 tablespoons peanut oil

½ teaspoon flaky sea salt

Special equipment: 8 wooden skewers, soaked in water for at least 2 hours

Cut the watermelon into 1-inch-thick pieces that are 2 inches long. Set aside. Grind the benne seeds, lemon verbena blossoms, fennel seeds, and cocoa powder in a mortar and pestle until the blossoms are roughly broken up and evenly incorporated into the mixture. (Alternatively, grind the mixture in a spice grinder.) Set aside.

Heat a gas or charcoal grill to high (450° to 500°F).

Thread a couple of watermelon pieces onto each skewer. Brush one side of the watermelon pieces evenly with the oil. Sprinkle each skewer evenly with about 2 teaspoons of the verbena salt. Place the skewers, oiled-side down, on the grill grates. Grill, uncovered and undisturbed, until grill marks form on the bottom, 2 to 3 minutes. Remove the watermelon skewers from the grill and arrange them, charred-side up, on a large platter. Sprinkle the watermelon evenly with flaky salt and the remaining verbena salt and serve.

VICTORY CHICKEN BURGERS

MAKES 4 BURGERS

On *A Different World*, a late-1980s sitcom set at the fictional Hillman College, the homecoming weekend episodes are the most memorable story lines. At the Pit, the campus café owned and managed by Vernon Gaines—played by the late Lou Myers—half-priced victory burgers were served during football games, and the Pit's ordering window, stuffed with bus buckets, was more than a place for laughs and french fries; it was self-affirming TV, at once aspirational and a time capsule of Black life. Because beef burgers are always on the cookout menu, I challenged myself to create a juicy chicken burger that's just as satisfying.

1 pound ground chicken

1 large egg

½ cup plain bread crumbs

1¼ teaspoons Chicken Salt (page 29)

2 teaspoons sherry vinegar

2 tablespoons peanut oil

4 slices white cheddar cheese

4 hamburger buns

Lettuce, tomato, pickles, ketchup, and/or mustard, for serving

Heat a gas or charcoal grill to medium-high (400°F). Move the coals to one side of the grill to make a cooler spot, if using a charcoal grill, or turn the flame down on one side if using a gas grill.

Combine the ground chicken, egg, bread crumbs, chicken salt, and sherry vinegar in a large bowl. Mix well with clean hands or a wooden spoon to combine, then form the mixture into 4 patties, about ½-inch thick, and set them on a plate. Refrigerate the burgers for 10 to 15 minutes.

Brush the chicken patties with the peanut oil and place them on the grill over direct heat. Close the grill lid and cook for 5 to 6 minutes per side, until the burgers reach 165°F on an instant-read thermometer. Move the burgers to the cooler side of the grill to avoid any flare-ups or if they're getting too charred. During the last 2 minutes of cooking, place a slice of cheese on top of the patties, close the grill lid again, and allow to melt.

Serve on hamburger buns with your favorite toppings.

FANCY MUSHROOMS

SERVES 3 TO 6

At the beginning of the global pandemic in 2020, I was growing mushrooms on my Flatbush, Brooklyn, rooftop (thanks to Smallhold grow kits). Time stood still, but the mushrooms grew. Mushrooms have become must-have fare on my cookout menu. Because mushrooms contain a surprising amount of water, when you cook them in a skillet you often end up steaming them rather than sautéing them as you intend. Grilling them avoids that problem and yields a richer flavor. Seasoning the mushrooms with a dry rub is what I enjoy best.

2 pounds large clusters of oyster, king trumpet, maitake, or lion's mane mushrooms

½ cup peanut oil

¼ cup Worcestershire sauce

¼ cup All-Purpose Seasoning (page 27)

Special equipment: vegetable grill basket

Heat a charcoal or gas grill to medium-high (400ºF).

Using a slightly damp kitchen towel, wipe the mushrooms to remove any dirt. Cut or tear the mushroom clusters into 6 large pieces, about the size of a hand. Place the mushrooms on a baking sheet and drizzle with the peanut oil and Worcestershire. Massage the seasoning into the mushrooms, being sure to get it into all the nooks and crannies.

Line a grill basket with foil and place it on the hot grill over direct heat. Add the mushrooms and cook, tossing with tongs occasionally, for 10 to 15 minutes, until browned and tender with crispy edges. Move the mushrooms away from any flare-ups if they are burning. Transfer to a baking sheet and serve warm.

TIP: I use a semi-damp paper towel or dish towel to clean mushrooms. Also, I advise that mushrooms be kept in an open brown paper bag on the countertop in a cool kitchen. If you aren't cooking them right away, storing in the not-so-cold part of the fridge works for a few days.

PORK RIBS

WITH A BBQ SAUCE FLIGHT

SERVES 4 TO 6

Right when New York City opened up after over a year of COVID-19 pandemic restrictions, I made my way to Blue Hill at Stone Barns in Tarrytown, New York, for pitmaster Bryan Furman's BBQ residency. The night was beautiful. We ate family-style, and alfresco; my guests were LaParis Phillips, a floral artist; Naïka Andre, an interior designer; and Syreeta Gates, iconoclast. Bryan created a variety of sauces for pulled pork. Just the thought of a specially curated flight of sauces brings traditional barbecue to a whole new level. This is my attempt to capture some of that flavor and magic.

4 pounds pork spareribs

1 tablespoon kosher salt

2 cups Peppercorn Rub (page 30)

SAUCES:

Fig Vinegar BBQ Sauce (page 33), for serving

Rhubarb BBQ Sauce (page 35)

NAT'S Red Hot Sauce (page 38)

Special equipment: hickory wood chips

Place the wood chips in a bucket and cover with cold water. Allow to soak overnight. Using a small knife, lift and remove the thin white membrane on the bone side of the rib rack. Rub the ribs with the salt and Peppercorn Rub. (This can be done up to a day ahead; store the ribs in a reusable storage bag.)

When you're ready to cook the ribs, heat a charcoal grill to medium-low (300ºF). Drain the wood chips and scatter a handful over the coals. Cover and wait until the wood chips start to smoke.

Place the ribs bone-side down on the not-blazing-hot side of the grill. Cover, with the lid vents open, and smoke the ribs for 15 minutes. Flip the ribs, cover, and smoke for another 15 minutes, then continue to cook the ribs until they reach an internal temperature of 165ºF on an instant-read thermometer, about an hour more, checking every 15 to 20 minutes. The minimum cook time is between 2 and 3 hours. Check the temperature of the grill periodically to ensure it remains between 275º and 300ºF, and move the ribs away from any hot spots or flare-ups. Add another handful of wood chips whenever the smoke dies down. Once fully cooked, the ribs should be tender, with the meat falling off the bone. Transfer the ribs to a baking sheet and cover with foil. Allow to rest for 10 minutes before slicing. Serve with the sauce.

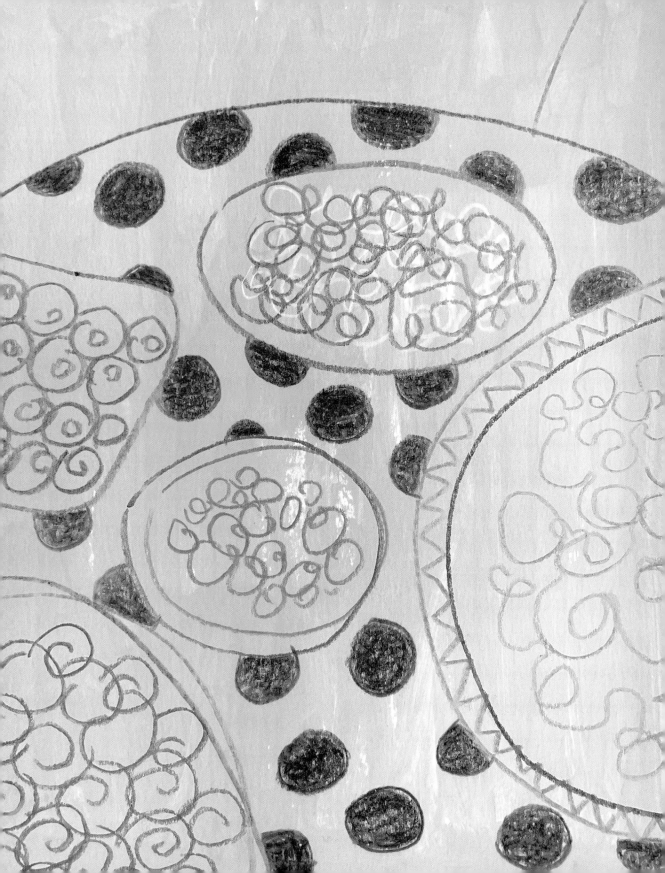

POTATO, GREEN & FRUIT SALADS

POTATO, GREEN & FRUIT SALADS

"Who made the potato salad?" is a universal statement uttered at least once at a Juneteenth gathering. Potato salad is the most revered African American cookout and barbecue side dish. It overshadows the rack of ribs; you can fight me on that point. Al Roker, the weatherman and TV personality, included a headnote in his 2002 *Big Bad Book of Barbecue* for a recipe titled "Deborah's Perry, Georgia, Potato Salad" (named after his wife, Deborah Roberts, an ABC news anchor and journalist), in which he flat-out says, "In the South, I think it's a criminal offense for there to be a barbecue without potato salad." Who wants just a plate of meat? One's mouth needs a break from chewing lamb chops and beef ribs.

inding out the potato salad maker isn't just a question of curiosity. Implied in the question is a statement: "I don't eat potato salad from just anybody." Supermarket deli cases are full of potato salad variations year-round. But come summertime, those sections are empty. People are buying potato salad for their barbecues and picnics. Please don't tell me you are the person buying the store-bought stuff; I'll let you in on a secret—we know. I think a just-right potato salad ought to be homemade and familiar. Those potato salad creations that contain cottage cheese, walnuts, green peas, or mashed avocado seem to me more abominations than variations. And don't get me started on raisins in potato salad.

I'm still a princess and learning from friends like Lynn Pitts, a native of Houma, Louisiana. Lynn, an advertising executive and writer, can roast the perfect Thanksgiving duck and bake a Marguerite cake (a bourbon cake, named after her late mother). She is, of course, potato salad royalty, too. My husband asks her to bring the potato to any cookout or BBQ we're hosting. Do you know what it means to be asked to bring the potato? You have been crowned. The family bows before you.

Lynn adds a bacon garnish to her potato salad; I'm with that technique. She uses Hellmann's mayo (not Duke's), boiled eggs, and scallions. In this cookbook, my potato salad recipe calls for bacon fat, sour cream, pickled banana peppers, and fresh parsley. Its base is peeled Yukon Golds. I hit flavor notes both creamy and bright. The best aim for some contrast: in *Rodney*

Scott's World of BBQ, the celebrated pitmaster writes, "I think it's the sweet-spicy-sour interplay between the sweet pickles, the mayonnaise, and the mustard that I like so much." Scott uses red potatoes, a few teaspoons of sugar, and pickle relish and shakes his signature rib rub on his potato salad. The man dedicated an entire chapter to salads.

From paprika, pickled peppers, or sweet pickles in potato salad to crumbled feta over cantaloupe, making a salad is an art. It's like visiting a museum and reading the object label; the eater wants to know the creative mind behind the dish, because the painting is not as simple as it looks. One can be adventurous—but balance is a must in any salad. The recipes that follow show how you might do just that. Please make more than one of these seasonal dishes for Juneteenth; a spread of sides is a sight to behold.

PLUM & SUPER GREENS PESTO SALAD

SERVES 8 TO 10

In the summer of 2017, I retreated to the kitchen to cook as therapy after experiencing a still-birth. According to the Centers for Disease Control, Black women are twice as likely to lose a child during pregnancy (at 20 weeks or beyond) than white and Hispanic women. The reasons behind this and other racial health disparities has lately become an area of much-needed study. Let's hope things change.

For me, food was the thing to lift me out of despair. I feel in control when I'm in the kitchen. And I feel creative. My mind can wander through the possibilities of various as-yet-untasted flavor combinations. That's better than thinking about all the complexities of losing a child. During that time, I made this dish. It has many layered memories, and is the best of who I am. It's not my mother's tossed salad. It's mine. And in those weeks after my misfortune, making something that was mine meant a lot.

1½ cups uncooked fonio or couscous (about 10 ounces)

3 tablespoons "everyday" olive oil

2¾ cups water

¾ teaspoon kosher salt

SUPER GREENS PESTO:

1 tablespoon plus 1¼ teaspoons kosher salt, plus more as needed

1 cup packed coarsely chopped stemmed collard green leaves (about 2 ounces)

1 cup packed coarsely chopped Swiss chard (leaves and stems)

¾ cup walnuts

½ ounce Parmesan cheese, grated on a Microplane (½ cup)

¼ teaspoon lime zest

1½ tablespoons fresh lime juice

1 teaspoon soy sauce

1 garlic clove, smashed and peeled

2 teaspoons honey

1 cup extra-virgin olive oil

¼ teaspoon freshly ground black pepper plus more as needed

2 pounds plums (about 5 medium), pitted and cut into ½-inch-thick wedges

In a medium saucepan, combine the fonio and the "everyday" olive oil and stir until coated. Add the water and salt. Bring to a boil over medium-high heat, then reduce the heat to low to maintain a simmer, cover, and cook for 1 minute. Remove from the heat and set aside to steam, still covered, for 5 minutes. Uncover the pot and fluff the fonio with a fork. Spread the fonio over a baking sheet to cool completely, about 45 minutes.

FOR THE PESTO: Meanwhile, bring a large pot of water to a boil over medium-high heat. Fill a large bowl with ice and water and set it next to the stove. Add 1 tablespoon of the salt and the collard greens and Swiss chard to the boiling water and blanch the collard greens and Swiss chard until bright green, about 2 minutes. Carefully transfer the collard greens and Swiss chard to the ice bath to stop the cooking. Drain the greens and pat completely dry. Set aside.

In a small dry skillet, toast the walnuts over medium heat until golden and fragrant, 4 to 5 minutes. Spread them over a cutting board and allow to cool for 5 minutes.

Coarsely chop ¼ cup of the walnuts and reserve them for garnish; transfer the remaining walnuts to a food processor and add the collards, Swiss chard, Parmesan, lime zest and juice, soy sauce, garlic, and 1 teaspoon of the honey. Pulse until a coarse paste forms, about 20 pulses. With the motor running, gradually stream in the extra-virgin olive oil until blended, about 45 seconds. Season with the pepper and ¾ teaspoon of the salt. Transfer the pesto to a small bowl and set aside.

In a large bowl, toss together the plums, the remaining 1 teaspoon honey, and ½ teaspoon salt. Set aside to macerate for 5 minutes.

To serve, spread 1½ cups of the pesto over a large platter. Top with the fonio and the plum mixture. Drizzle with the remaining pesto and garnish with the reserved walnuts and more freshly ground pepper.

SOUTHERN-ISH POTATO SALAD

SERVES 6 TO 8

The greatest failure when making potato salad is overcooking the spuds—creamy mashed potatoes is a no-go for any potato salad recipe. You want a waxy variety like fingerlings, Yukon Golds, or red potatoes; these varieties will keep their shape and texture when cooked right. Bobby Seale, cofounder of the Black Panther Party, said it well in his 1988 cookbook *Barbeque'n with Bobby*, where he wrote under a recipe titled "Hunky Crunchy Potato Salad" that his mother's potato salad was a "tasty quasi-mashed potato salad." My pro tip is to season the potatoes while they are warm. Begin your training to be a queen.

3 pounds Yukon Gold potatoes, peeled and cut into 1-inch pieces

⅓ cup plus 2 teaspoons kosher salt

8 ounces bacon (optional)

About 4 tablespoons (½ stick) unsalted butter (if omitting the bacon)

1 medium yellow onion, chopped

1 fennel bulb, cored and chopped

¼ cup extra-virgin olive oil

½ cup sour cream

¼ cup fresh parsley leaves and stems, chopped, plus 2 tablespoons leaves for garnish

2 teaspoons ground mustard

1 teaspoon smoked paprika, plus extra for garnish

Zest of 2 lemons (2 tablespoons)

3 tablespoons Quick-Pickled Banana Pepper brine (page 44)

¼ teaspoon freshly ground black pepper

Peel your potatoes and rinse in cold water. Place the potatoes in a large pot and add water to cover (around 10 cups) and ⅓ cup of the salt. Bring to a boil over high heat and cook the potatoes, uncovered, until just tender but with some bite still, 18 to 25 minutes. Be sure not to overcook the potatoes—you don't want mushy potato salad! Drain the potatoes and transfer to a large bowl. Sprinkle with 1 teaspoon of the salt and allow to cool for 30 minutes or so.

continued on page 150

Southern-ish Potato Salad, *continued*

Meanwhile, in a large skillet, cook the bacon (if using) over medium heat until the fat is rendered and the bacon is crisp and browned, 7 to 10 minutes. Transfer to a paper towel–lined plate, leaving the fat in the pan. (If you're omitting the bacon, melt the butter in a large skillet here.) Add the onion and fennel to the hot bacon fat in the skillet and cook until softened, about 5 minutes. Season with the remaining 1 teaspoon of salt. Remove from the heat and allow to cool.

Add the cooled fennel mixture to the bowl with the potatoes, then add the olive oil, sour cream, chopped parsley, ground mustard, paprika, lemon zest, pickled banana pepper brine, and pepper and stir to combine. Taste! Taste! If necessary, you may need to add a tad more of the seasonings and sour cream. Garnish with the parsley leaves and, if desired, an extra pinch of paprika.

We're talking about potato salad here, so: everyone has their way. Some people make it the day of; some people make it the day ahead. Store in the refrigerator until ready to serve.

NEW AGE WEDGE

SERVES 4

Iceberg lettuce never went out of style. Yes, the produce aisles and farmers' markets are brimming with arugula, Little Gem lettuce, endive, and mixed greens, but iceberg's crispness and crunch make it classic.

The wedge salad is a classic preparation of this classic lettuce. I'd describe the wedge as a restaurant starter. Bone-in rib eye steaks and succulent salmon fillets cooked at home deserve restaurant treatment, and so, too, does this salad. Fill a giant bar cart with plates of wedges for your guests. I've played with tradition here and added brandied grapes. Chef Kaylah Thomas was my co-conspirator for a Juneteenth terrace party in 2019. She suggested replacing baby tomatoes with soaked grapes. That day I soaked the grapes in Seedlip nonalcoholic spirits; mostly, though, I use brandy. A version of this dish was served at Zingerman's Roadhouse (an Ann Arbor, Michigan, institution) in 2019, when I was a guest speaker at the restaurant during Black History Month.

HERBED-INFUSED BREAD CRUMBS:

1½ cups fresh bread crumbs

5 tablespoons coarsely chopped fresh herbs (a mix of cilantro, parsley, and basil leaves)

2 tablespoons "everyday" olive oil

¼ teaspoon kosher salt

BRANDIED GRAPES AND GRAPE BRANDY DRESSING:

1 bunch red grapes (2 cups), removed from the stems

1 cup brandy

¼ cup rice vinegar

¼ cup extra-virgin olive oil

½ teaspoon kosher salt

¼ teaspoon freshly ground black pepper

WEDGE SALAD:

1 head iceberg lettuce, cut into 4 wedges

½ cup Quick-Pickled Red Onions (page 45)

½ cup crumbled blue cheese, for garnish

Cracked black pepper

FOR THE HERBED-INFUSED BREAD CRUMBS: Preheat the oven to 400ºF.

In a large bowl, combine the bread crumbs, herbs, "everyday" olive oil, and salt and toss to combine. Spread evenly over a baking sheet and toast in the oven for 7 to 8 minutes, stirring halfway through, until golden and fragrant. Remove from the oven and allow to cool completely. (The bread crumbs will keep in an airtight container in a cool, dry place for 3 to 4 days.)

continued on page 153

New Age Wedge, *continued*

FOR THE BRANDIED GRAPES AND DRESSING: Put the grapes in an airtight container, add the brandy, and cover. Soak in the refrigerator for a couple of hours or preferably overnight. (The brandied grapes will keep in an airtight container in the refrigerator for up to 5 days.)

Drain the grapes, reserving ¼ cup of the soaking liquid, and set aside for the salad.

In a small bowl, whisk together the reserved ¼ cup grape soaking liquid, the vinegar, and the extra-virgin olive oil to combine. Season with the salt and pepper. Set aside.

FOR THE WEDGE SALAD: On a platter or individual plates, arrange the wedges of iceberg lettuce. Sprinkle with the brandy-soaked grapes, bread crumbs, ½ cup of the pickled onions, and a drizzle of the dressing. Garnish with a sprinkle of blue cheese and serve with additional cracked black pepper.

WHISK AWAY

Back when I bought store-bought dressing, Paul Newman's brand was the dressing that sat in my shopping cart.

I've been making homemade salad dressings for more than twenty years. In this chapter, you have a range of salad dressings, from creamy to tangy. These compositions, from buttermilk to oregano, work perfectly for a big bowl of romaine, drizzled on a grain bowl, or as a dip for farmer's garden vegetables. Store these dressings and the pesto in an airtight container in the refrigerator for up to 1 week.

CARROTS & MUSTARD FLOWERS

SERVES 4

Mustard greens belong to the brassica family, making them cousins of cabbage and Brussels sprouts. They are a bit spicier than either of their kin, though. You're most likely to find them at farm stands or farmers' markets; substitute broccoli rabe florets here if you can't.

3 pounds carrots

2 tablespoons "everyday" olive oil

1 bunch flowering mustard greens, stemmed

ONION-MUSTARD DRESSING (MAKES 1¾ CUPS DRESSING):

½ cup fresh orange juice (from 2 oranges)

½ cup extra-virgin olive oil

½ teaspoon kosher salt

1 teaspoon freshly ground black pepper

½ teaspoon mustard seeds, crushed

¼ cup sour cream

2 teaspoons apple cider vinegar

1 small shallot, finely chopped

Preheat the oven to 400ºF. On a baking sheet, toss the carrots with the "everyday" olive oil. Roast the carrots for 25 to 30 minutes, shaking the pan periodically, until golden and tender.

FOR THE ONION-MUSTARD DRESSING: Meanwhile, in a small bowl, whisk together the orange juice and extra-virgin olive oil until well combined; season with salt, black pepper, and mustard seeds. Then whisk in the sour cream, apple cider vinegar, and chopped shallot. Stir together until combined.

When the carrots have finished roasting, allow them to cool for 5 to 10 minutes, then thinly slice them on an angle and place in a large bowl.

Reserve a few flowering tops of the mustard greens for garnish. Toss the carrot slices with the remaining mustard greens in the large bowl. Drizzle the dressing around the rim of the bowl and toss to evenly coat. Place the salad on a large platter and drizzle more dressing on top. Finish with the reserved mustard green flowers.

SUMMER PEAS, GREEN BEANS & CORN SALAD

SERVES 10 TO 12

In my American South, fresh shelled lady peas, crowders, cream peas—delicate and pearl-shaped—show up at the neighborhood market as a welcome sign of summer. But frozen varieties of these delicious peas are so much more common that I have taken to making mental notes of where I can use them. At the Forsyths Farmers' Market in Savannah, Georgia, Joseph Fields Farms sells shelled peas in sealed storage bags, sitting in iced coolers. Farmview Market, a local food emporium located in Eatonton, Georgia, stocks their varieties in a refrigerated section alongside Rock House Creamery buttermilk. When I'm in Athens, I stop by Bell's Food Store, a family-owned store and country-cooking emporium.

SALAD:

¼ cup kosher salt

3 cups shelled southern peas, like fresh crowders or lady peas

3 cups fresh corn kernels (from 2 to 3 cobs)

2 cups halved green beans (cut in half on an angle)

4 celery ribs, thinly sliced, leaves reserved

1 cup chopped red bell pepper

1 small red onion, thinly sliced

BUTTERMILK DRESSING:

2 tablespoons sherry vinegar

2 garlic cloves, grated

2 tablespoons honey

¼ teaspoon freshly ground black pepper

1 tablespoon fresh thyme

1 cup full-fat buttermilk, well shaken

½ cup sour cream

⅓ cup extra-virgin olive oil

¼ teaspoon kosher salt

Leaves from 2 sprigs thyme, for garnish

FOR THE SALAD: Bring a large pot of water to a boil over medium-high heat and add the salt. Fill a large bowl with ice and water and set it next to the

continued on page 158

TOMATO & EGGPLANT SALAD

SERVES 4

The elegance of Sungolds, Cherokee Purples, Citrines, and Green Zebras reminds me of the elegance captured so well by the late fashion model and media mogul B. Smith on the cover of her cookbook *Rituals & Celebrations*. A poised B. stands in front of a body of water near a table with multicolored flowers and dinnerware trimmed in blue. I remember eating solo at her iconic restaurant on my first adult trip to DC; I felt so fancy. Just like B. Smith, this salad is timeless. There were no tomatoes in her cover photo, but a color mix of heirloom tomatoes can be as beautiful and welcome an addition to a table as a bouquet.

OREGANO OIL (MAKES ½ CUP):

1 garlic clove, peeled

¼ cup fresh oregano leaves

½ cup extra-virgin olive oil

1 teaspoon kosher salt

SALAD:

2 pounds baby or Fairy Tale eggplants, or
4 small eggplants, cut into ½-inch-thick slices

3 tablespoons "everyday" olive oil

1 teaspoon kosher salt, plus more as needed

½ cup fresh mozzarella bocconcini, or
1 (8-ounce) ball fresh mozzarella

1 pint baby heirloom tomatoes, halved

Leaves from 2 sprigs oregano

FOR THE OREGANO OIL: In a food processor, combine the garlic, oregano leaves, and extra-virgin olive oil and process until smooth and combined. Season with the salt.

FOR THE SALAD: Preheat the oven to 400ºF. Place the eggplant slices on a baking sheet in a single layer. Brush with the "everyday" olive oil and season with the salt. Roast for 30 minutes, turning the eggplant over halfway through, until golden brown and tender. Remove from the oven and allow to cool. When the eggplant slices are cooled, cut them into ½-inch pieces and set aside.

Cut the bocconcini in half; if using a mozzarella ball, cut the ball in half and then into thin half-moons. Arrange the eggplant, mozzarella, and tomatoes on a platter and drizzle with ¼ cup of the oregano oil. Sprinkle the fresh oregano leaves on top and serve.

CRAB & EGG SALAD

SERVES 4 TO 6

This salad was somewhat of a mistake. During the promotion of my first cookbook, the zine *Put A Egg On It* hosted a dinner party for their readers in a spacious loft in New York City's Chelsea neighborhood. I started prepping trout deviled eggs at home, but the eggs were too fresh (lots of master home cooks say the older the egg, the easier to peel). I had a bowl of jaggedly peeled eggs, and on the fly, Jenn de la Vega, recipe developer and longtime friend, suggested chopping them, mixing the ingredients, and slathering over toasted bread. This salad could be a standalone appetizer. Bingo! It worked. This salad plays off similar elements: fish, eggs, creaminess.

3 large eggs

¼ cup mayonnaise

½ cup sour cream

¼ teaspoon red pepper flakes

¼ teaspoon smoked paprika

½ teaspoon balsamic vinegar

½ teaspoon kosher salt, plus more for finishing

¼ teaspoon freshly cracked black pepper, plus more for finishing

1 teaspoon ground mustard

¼ cup fresh parsley, finely chopped

8 ounces lump crabmeat

Put the eggs in a medium saucepan and add cold water to cover. Bring to a boil over high heat. Hard-boiled eggs take around 10 minutes. Place a lid on the saucepan and remove from the heat. Let cool for about 10 minutes, then transfer to a bowl of cold water and peel.

Slice the hard-boiled eggs into quarters and place them in a medium bowl. Add the mayo, sour cream, red pepper flakes, paprika, vinegar, salt, black pepper, ground mustard, and parsley and stir to combine. Gently fold in the crabmeat. Taste! Adjust the salt and pepper, if desired, and serve.

NOTE: I buy premium lump crabmeat that has been pasteurized. Most super-markets sell it near the seafood aisle.

TOMATO & EGGPLANT SALAD

SERVES 4

The elegance of Sungolds, Cherokee Purples, Citrines, and Green Zebras reminds me of the elegance captured so well by the late fashion model and media mogul B. Smith on the cover of her cookbook *Rituals & Celebrations*. A poised B. stands in front of a body of water near a table with multicolored flowers and dinnerware trimmed in blue. I remember eating solo at her iconic restaurant on my first adult trip to DC; I felt so fancy. Just like B. Smith, this salad is timeless. There were no tomatoes in her cover photo, but a color mix of heirloom tomatoes can be as beautiful and welcome an addition to a table as a bouquet.

OREGANO OIL (MAKES ½ CUP):

1 garlic clove, peeled

¼ cup fresh oregano leaves

½ cup extra-virgin olive oil

1 teaspoon kosher salt

SALAD:

**2 pounds baby or Fairy Tale eggplants, or
4 small eggplants, cut into ½-inch-thick slices**

3 tablespoons "everyday" olive oil

1 teaspoon kosher salt, plus more as needed

**½ cup fresh mozzarella bocconcini, or
1 (8-ounce) ball fresh mozzarella**

1 pint baby heirloom tomatoes, halved

Leaves from 2 sprigs oregano

FOR THE OREGANO OIL: In a food processor, combine the garlic, oregano leaves, and extra-virgin olive oil and process until smooth and combined. Season with the salt.

FOR THE SALAD: Preheat the oven to 400ºF. Place the eggplant slices on a baking sheet in a single layer. Brush with the "everyday" olive oil and season with the salt. Roast for 30 minutes, turning the eggplant over halfway through, until golden brown and tender. Remove from the oven and allow to cool. When the eggplant slices are cooled, cut them into ½-inch pieces and set aside.

Cut the bocconcini in half; if using a mozzarella ball, cut the ball in half and then into thin half-moons. Arrange the eggplant, mozzarella, and tomatoes on a platter and drizzle with ¼ cup of the oregano oil. Sprinkle the fresh oregano leaves on top and serve.

SUMMER PEAS, GREEN BEANS & CORN SALAD

SERVES 10 TO 12

In my American South, fresh shelled lady peas, crowders, cream peas—delicate and pearl-shaped—show up at the neighborhood market as a welcome sign of summer. But frozen varieties of these delicious peas are so much more common that I have taken to making mental notes of where I can use them. At the Forsyths Farmers' Market in Savannah, Georgia, Joseph Fields Farms sells shelled peas in sealed storage bags, sitting in iced coolers. Farmview Market, a local food emporium located in Eatonton, Georgia, stocks their varieties in a refrigerated section alongside Rock House Creamery buttermilk. When I'm in Athens, I stop by Bell's Food Store, a family-owned store and country-cooking emporium.

SALAD:

¼ cup kosher salt

3 cups shelled southern peas, like fresh crowders or lady peas

3 cups fresh corn kernels (from 2 to 3 cobs)

2 cups halved green beans (cut in half on an angle)

4 celery ribs, thinly sliced, leaves reserved

1 cup chopped red bell pepper

1 small red onion, thinly sliced

BUTTERMILK DRESSING:

2 tablespoons sherry vinegar

2 garlic cloves, grated

2 tablespoons honey

¼ teaspoon freshly ground black pepper

1 tablespoon fresh thyme

1 cup full-fat buttermilk, well shaken

½ cup sour cream

⅓ cup extra-virgin olive oil

¼ teaspoon kosher salt

Leaves from 2 sprigs thyme, for garnish

FOR THE SALAD: Bring a large pot of water to a boil over medium-high heat and add the salt. Fill a large bowl with ice and water and set it next to the

continued on page 158

Summer Peas, Green Beans & Corn Salad, *continued*

stove. Cook the southern peas in the boiling water for about 25 minutes, or until creamy inside but not mushy, then remove using a mesh sieve and immediately transfer to the ice bath to stop the cooking.

Blanch the corn, then the green beans, blanching each for 2 minutes, then transferring to the ice bath. Drain the beans, corn, and lady peas in a colander and set aside to cool completely.

In a large bowl, combine the cooled bean mixture, the celery, bell pepper, and onion. Cover and chill in the refrigerator until ready to serve.

FOR THE BUTTERMILK DRESSING: In a medium bowl, whisk together the vinegar, garlic, honey, black pepper, and thyme until well combined. While whisking, slowly stream in the buttermilk, then the sour cream, and then the olive oil, whisking until emulsified and smooth. Season with the salt.

Before serving, drizzle ¼ cup of the dressing around the rim of the bowl and toss to combine. Add more dressing, if you like, and garnish with the reserved celery leaves and the fresh thyme.

CANTALOUPE & FETA

SERVES 4 TO 6

When it comes to fruit salads, let the fruit shine. Shop for high-quality produce, almost at its peak. Your honeydew and cantaloupe should be slightly soft to the touch and smell sweet. Unlike watermelon, cantaloupe and honeydew will continue to sweeten and improve off the vine. Just don't wait so long that they become mushy. A melon baller is equivalent to a mini ice cream scoop without the release mechanism. It can turn out glistening rounds of honeydew and cantaloupe with ease. There is a dance to piling balls of melon in a structural bowl. I keep the Isley Brothers, PJ Morton, and James Blake playing when I'm making melon spheres. Choose whatever makes you groove. If you don't have a melon baller, cubing the honeydew makes for an interesting visual and textural contrast to the round cantaloupe balls.

3 cups cantaloupe balls (formed using a melon baller)

1 cup honeydew balls (formed using a melon baller)

1¾ teaspoons lime zest (from about 2 limes)

¼ cup crumbled feta cheese

¼ teaspoon chili powder

In a large bowl, toss the cantaloupe and honeydew with the lime zest. Spread over a large platter and sprinkle with the feta and the chili powder. Serve chilled.

SNOW CONES, ICE POP'S & ICE CREAM

SNOW CONES, ICE POPS & ICE CREAM

Throughout the 1920s, Solomon Sir Jones, an African American minister and filmmaker born in Tennessee, masterfully recorded Black life in the American South and Midwest, and in Europe. One black-and-white silent film shot in 1925 shows American flags raised high in a Beaumont, Texas, Juneteenth parade. Groups of children strut down the street in identical Girl and Boy Scout–like uniforms, tight-waisted crisp cotton midi dresses; the women watch, wearing adorned hats that look like flower-dotted desserts. These kinds of public Juneteenth events showed a particular Black patriotism.

Although I didn't attend a public Juneteenth event in 2021, my Juneteenth party that year was special, a dose of Americana—a time to rejoice just being alive, punctuated by ice cream. With the COVID-19 vaccine to protect us, my friends and I gathered outside.

Along with my own family, we were joined by Erika Council, founder of Bomb Biscuit Co. and granddaughter of the late Mama Dip, chef-owner of the beloved Mama Dip's Kitchen in Chapel Hill, North Carolina, as well as Erika's husband and kids. I can't remember the exact moment I met Erika, but every time we connect, it's over good food. I hosted a traditional cookout, with fiery, off-menu sausages (hot links) from Ryan Smith's Staplehouse in Atlanta. Erika made the potato salad, and it looked, tasted, and was packaged like it was made by a person who always brings the potato salad, in a large plastic container with a cover that doesn't smash the top. We ended the evening with a swoon-worthy ice cream sundae: luscious vanilla ice cream swirled with pieces of doughnut and topped with whipped cream, spoonfuls of strawberry compote, and shreds of lime zest.

Whether you're a teeny tot or an old bird, we all stay ready for the chilled ice cream cookie or the snow cone topped with crushed peppercorns at the end of a meal. There's no time for talk of calories and indulgences. Given all the complications that come packaged up with being Black in America, the pleasures of an ice cream dessert require no regrets. It has been earned.

CUCUMBER GRANITA

SERVES 6

I was inspired to make granita after watching my friend Benjamin "BJ" Dennis, chef and Gullah Geechee cultural bearer, serve this easy and refreshing after-dinner treat for his private clients. It was a fitting finale to the richly seasoned goodness of his cuisine. Granita, widely known as a Sicilian dessert, is a combination of fruit, sugar, and water, frozen until set. The key to smooth granita is running your fork through the mixture a few times while it's in the freezer.

½ cup sugar

½ cup water

2 teaspoons lime zest, plus extra for garnish

2 tablespoons fresh lime juice

4 cups cubed cucumbers (about 2 large)

½ teaspoon kosher salt

6 sprigs dill

Combine the sugar and water in a small saucepan and bring to a boil over medium-high heat. Cook, stirring, until the sugar is completely dissolved, about 1 minute. Immediately remove from the heat.

Transfer the sugar mixture to a high-speed blender or food processor and add the lime zest and juice, cucumber, and salt. Blend until smooth, about 30 seconds.

Pour the mixture into a 9 x 5-inch loaf pan or baking sheet. Freeze in 45-minute increments, dragging a fork through to mix and break up large chunks after each time, until a frozen and fluffy ice mixture forms, 6 to 8 hours total.

To serve, divide the granita among six dishes and garnish each with a sprig of dill and a sprinkling of lime zest.

HIBISCUS SICHUAN SNOW CONES

MAKES 6 TO 8

Pulling out my snow cone maker changes the whole mood of my house—even the toddler tantrums cease. It's a magical appliance that draws people to it as they watch the snow cones being made. For my Juneteenth celebrations, I shave mounds of fluffy ice and make a big batch of thick syrup to mix into different flavors—red (hibiscus), purple (purple sweet potato), and yellow (marigold). The fluffy ice gets drenched with the colorful syrups, then topped with whipped cream and edible flowers or spices. To punch things up, add 1 ounce of vodka to a snow cone and eat with a spoon. A good snow cone tray works well when serving a crowd.

HIBISCUS SICHUAN SYRUP:

1 cup water

1½ cups dried hibiscus flowers (1½ ounces)

1 tablespoon whole Sichuan peppercorns

¼ teaspoon fine sea salt

2 cups sugar

WHIPPED CREAM (OPTIONAL):

½ cup chilled heavy cream

2 teaspoons confectioners' sugar

6 to 8 cups shaved ice (use a snow cone maker)

Crushed Sichuan peppercorns, for garnish

Edible flowers, for garnish

Special equipment: snow cone maker, paper snow cone cups

FOR THE HIBISCUS SICHUAN SYRUP: In a medium saucepan, combine the water, hibiscus flowers, Sichuan peppercorns, salt, and sugar and bring to a boil over medium-high heat. Reduce the heat to medium-low and cook, stirring occasionally, until the syrup is thickened slightly, about 20 minutes. Remove from the heat and allow to cool to room temperature, about 1 hour.

continued on page 174

Hibiscus Sichuan Snow Cones, *continued*

Strain the hibiscus mixture through a fine-mesh sieve into a medium measuring cup, firmly pressing the hibiscus flowers against the sieve using the back of a spoon to get all the liquid out. Discard the flowers and other solids. Add water to the hibiscus syrup as needed to yield 1½ cups liquid. If possible, transfer the mixture to a squeeze bottle for easy dispensing. Store in the refrigerator until ready to use for the snow cones, up to several weeks. Allow the syrup to come to room temperature before using.

FOR THE WHIPPED CREAM: In the clean bowl of a stand mixer fitted with the whisk attachment or in a large bowl using a handheld mixer, beat the heavy cream and sugar on medium-high speed until the cream is doubled in volume and medium-stiff peaks have formed. Chill in the refrigerator until ready to serve.

Divide the shaved ice evenly among six to eight 6-ounce paper snow cone cups. Drizzle each snow cone with 3 to 4 tablespoons of the hibiscus syrup (reserve the remaining syrup for more snow cones). Top each snow cone with about 1 tablespoon of the whipped cream (if using) and garnish with crushed Sichuan peppercorns and/or edible flowers.

NOTE: These snow cones can also be made with purple sweet potatoes; just substitute purple sweet potatoes for the orange-fleshed ones in the Sweet Potato Syrup recipe on page 69. Marigold snow cones can be made using the Marigold Syrup on page 59. Switching out the Sichuan peppercorns for pink peppercorns in the hibiscus syrup is another option.

LIBERATION SUNDAE

MAKES 4

On February 5, 1960, a protest movement was born at Atlanta's Milton & Yates Drugstore soda fountain. That movement was eventually led by the Committee on Appeal for Human Rights (COAHR), a group of students from Morehouse College, Clark College, Atlanta University, Spelman College, Morris Brown College, and the Interdenominational Theological Center. These institutions are collectively known as the Atlanta University Center. COAHR met in campus halls, local businesses, and restaurants. They drafted a strategic plan to use sit-ins to chop down segregation in the capital of the south—Atlanta. This is my ode to my alma mater, Clark Atlanta University, and college students who were inspired by the civil rights lunch counter protests in Greensboro, North Carolina—and sparked a better America.

8 scoops Dairy-Free Chocolate Sorbet (recipe follows)

1 cup Rhubarb Compote (recipe follows)

4 sprigs chocolate mint, for garnish

Place 2 scoops of chocolate sorbet into each of four sundae glasses or bowls. Evenly top with the compote and garnish each with a sprig of chocolate mint. Serve.

DAIRY-FREE CHOCOLATE SORBET

MAKES 3 CUPS

I've made a habit of stashing vegan or vegetarian options in the corner of my freezer. I tend to whip together decadent vegan sundaes on the fly that taste as rich and satisfying as milk-based desserts. My goal is to please all my guests, omnivores, vegans, and vegetarians alike.

2 cups water

1 cup packed dark brown sugar

½ cup unsweetened cocoa powder

8 ounces dark chocolate, finely chopped

1 teaspoon coffee liqueur (see Tip)

¼ teaspoon sea salt

Special equipment: ice cream maker

If using an ice cream maker with a freezer bowl, it'll need to be frozen for at least 12 hours before using.

Bring the water to a boil in a medium saucepan over medium-high heat. Whisk in the brown sugar and cook for 1 minute, stirring to dissolve the sugar, then reduce the heat to medium-low. Whisk in the cocoa powder until well combined. Remove the saucepan from the heat and add the chocolate. Whisk until the chocolate is melted and the mixture is smooth and incorporated. Allow the mixture to cool for 10 minutes, then stir in the coffee liqueur and salt.

Strain the mixture through a fine-mesh sieve into a 9 x 5-inch loaf pan. Cover and chill in the refrigerator for at least 1 hour, until completely cold.

Whisk the chilled chocolate mixture again. Use an immersion blender (or transfer to a standing blender and blend) to break up any solids. Pour the liquid into the frozen ice cream maker bowl and churn into sorbet according to the manufacturer's instructions. Transfer the sorbet to an airtight plastic container and freeze for 2 to 4 hours to set.

The sorbet can be stored in the freezer for up to 2 weeks. If it's too frozen to scoop, let it stand at room temperature for 10 to 15 minutes to soften, then serve.

TIP: This recipe requires a super small amount of coffee liqueur. If you are open to investing in an entire bottle, buy St. George coffee liqueur. Or you can make your own by combining the following in a medium saucepan: 1 cup sugar, 1 cup water, 1 cup vodka, ¼ cup cold coffee, and 2 splashes of vanilla extract. Bring to a simmer over medium-high heat and cook until the sugar is dissolved. Allow to cool to room temperature. Store in an airtight container in the refrigerator for several weeks.

RHUBARB COMPOTE

MAKES 2 CUPS

Listen good: This compote is terrific with ice cream for dessert, but make extra and spoon it onto full-fat yogurt for breakfast or spread it on toast with ricotta for lunch.

2 pounds rhubarb, ends trimmed, cut into 3-inch pieces

1½ cups sugar

1 teaspoon red pepper flakes

1 cinnamon stick

½ teaspoon kosher salt

½ teaspoon freshly grated nutmeg

Preheat the oven to 400°F.

Toss the rhubarb, sugar, red pepper flakes, cinnamon stick, salt, and nutmeg on a baking sheet until well combined. Spread into an even layer. Cover the baking sheet with foil and roast for about 10 minutes, or until the rhubarb just begins to release some juices. Remove the foil and roast for another 10 to 15 minutes, until the sauce is bubbling and syrupy and the rhubarb can be easily pierced with a fork. Allow to cool completely and discard the cinnamon stick. Store in an airtight container in the refrigerator for up to 1 week.

CHOCOLATE MINT

Every year, I plant a windowsill garden and cross my fingers for success. When I travel for more than three days, all hell breaks loose; either my plant sitter mishandles the watering, or the rising room temperature wilts my delicate herbs. No worries at all in the end, because I can rely on Athens' Daily Groceries Co-op, Brooklyn's Greene Grape Provisions, or a farmers' market for fresh mint. Whether homegrown or store-bought, fresh chocolate mint adds a liveliness to this dish that tastes nothing like the flavor of the peppermint candies or mint tea we're all so used to. It's a game changer.

RASPBERRY YOGURT POPS

MAKES 6 POPS

In New Orleans, they called them frozen cups or hucklebucks, and New Orleans singer Wanda Rouzan named her record label after them. In Savannah, chef Mashama Bailey knew them as "thrills," and she's created a cheffy version of them for the menu at her restaurant. Whatever you call them, Black women across the South sold some version of Kool-Aid or fruit juice, frozen in their freezers and available for a couple of nickels or dimes. At the peak of summer, I'm determined to process ripe fruit right away for fear my farmers' market bounty will go bad. I make quick decisions about usage, and often mix up these yogurt pops. Raspberries tend to get moldy spots if not appropriately handled. Store the berries in the refrigerator soon after you purchase them, and don't rinse them until you're ready to eat them or use them.

1¼ cups fresh raspberries

6 tablespoons sugar

¼ teaspoon kosher salt

2 cups plain full-fat Greek yogurt

¼ cup chilled heavy cream

Special equipment: ice pop molds

In a medium bowl, combine the raspberries, 3 tablespoons of the sugar, and the salt and mash using a fork or potato masher until the mixture is broken down but not super smooth. Set aside to macerate for 10 to 15 minutes.

In a medium bowl, stir together the yogurt, cream, and remaining 3 tablespoons sugar.

Fill the ice pop molds with the yogurt and the raspberry mash, adding them in alternating spoonfuls until the molds are filled. Use a skewer or ice pop stick to swirl the mixture in the molds. Cover and freeze for 5 to 6 hours, until frozen solid.

If the ice pops do not slide out easily, run the bottom of the molds under warm water for up to 10 seconds to loosen them.

ROASTED NECTARINE SUNDAE

MAKES 4

In 2019, I stepped into the High Museum of Art to see the late Virgil Abloh's exhibit titled *Figures of Speech*. Virgil was probably best known as the creative director of Louis Vuitton menswear and founder of the streetwear label Off-White. This retrospective traced the Chicago kid's unconventional rise from architect to fashion industry icon. Just as his fashion incorporates the street aesthetic and all the finer touches he learned, this sundae takes the basic and makes it special. It's opulent, yet brings to mind Dairy Queen's Peanut Buster Parfait. Fashion inspires my Juneteenth desserts and helps to define my vision of Black leisure. Like those casual outfits that folks quietly labor over so they can look effortlessly stylish at the Juneteenth party, this dessert incorporates a few fancy flourishes but is still a throwback to simpler food memories.

ROASTED NECTARINES:

1 teaspoon ground cardamom

½ cup packed light brown sugar

½ teaspoon sea salt

8 ripe nectarines, halved and pitted

8 tablespoons (1 stick) unsalted butter, cut into cubes

8 scoops Honey Vanilla Ice Cream (recipe follows), for serving

Pistachio Brittle (page 186), crushed, for serving

Caramel Sauce (recipe follows), drizzled, for serving

FOR THE ROASTED NECTARINES: Adjust an oven rack to be about 5 inches away from the broiler heat element and preheat the broiler to high.

Combine the cardamom, brown sugar, and salt in a small ramekin. Place the nectarines cut-side up in a single layer on a baking sheet. Dot the nectarines with the butter and sprinkle with the brown sugar mixture. Broil for 7 to 10

continued on page 184

Roasted Nectarine Sundae, *continued*

minutes, until golden brown and caramelized, basting with the juices from the baking sheet halfway through using a spoon or heat-resistant brush. Remove from the oven. Pour the liquid from the baking sheet into a measuring cup and reserve for the caramel sauce; set the nectarines aside to cool.

Add enough butter to the pan juices reserved from the nectarines to make 6 tablespoons total. Transfer to a small bowl and set aside.

To assemble the sundae, place 2 generous scoops of vanilla ice cream in a bowl, top with the roasted nectarines, and garnish with crushed pistachio brittle. Drizzle with the caramel sauce and serve.

CARAMEL SAUCE

MAKES 2 CUPS

If the term "à la mode" hadn't already been applied to ice cream toppings, I think it would be good to apply it to caramel sauce. It's such a rich, indulgent topping that will sit well with just about any dessert. You can buy jarred caramel sauce and, I admit, I have. But the fresh butter and cream in a homemade sauce make all the difference.

2 cups granulated sugar

1 cup heavy cream, at room temperature

2 teaspoons sea salt

Up to 12 tablespoons (1 stick) salted butter, cubed, at room temperature

In a heavy saucepan, heat the sugar over medium heat. It will form clumps and eventually melt into a brown liquid; be mindful that it does not burn. Add the pan juice butter (6 tablespoons) plus 6 more tablespoons butter in chunks and stir to combine, watching for splatter. If it fails to incorporate, lift the pan off the heat and stir until it does. Once all the butter has been incorporated, allow the mixture to bubble, undisturbed, for 1 minute. Slowly add the cream, being careful of any sputtering, and stir. Allow to bubble again for 1 minute, then remove from the heat and season with the salt. Transfer to an airtight container and set aside until ready to use; it will thicken as it cools. (The caramel sauce can be stored in the refrigerator for up to 1 week.)

HONEY VANILLA ICE CREAM

MAKES 1 QUART

Made-from-scratch honey vanilla is a pleasure worth waiting those extra few minutes for. It doesn't take a lot of honey to make this dish stand out from the usual vanilla ice cream. Even if the honey is too subtle to identify, you know there's something a little different at work here.

5 large egg yolks

6 tablespoons whole milk

1¾ cups heavy cream

½ cup sugar

¼ teaspoon coarse salt

2 teaspoons honey

2 teaspoons vanilla extract

Special equipment: ice cream maker

If using an ice cream maker with a freezer bowl, it'll need to be frozen for at least 12 hours before using.

In a medium bowl, whisk the egg yolks until smooth; set aside.

In a medium saucepan, combine the milk, cream, sugar, and salt and place over medium-high heat. Heat the milk mixture, whisking continuously and watching it carefully—you don't want this mixture to boil—until the sugar is dissolved, 2 to 3 minutes, reducing the heat if you notice rapid bubbles. Reduce the heat to medium-low.

While whisking continuously, slowly pour about 1 cup of the milk mixture into the bowl of egg yolks to temper them and whisk to combine. Pour the egg yolk mixture into the saucepan with the remaining milk mixture and cook, whisking, until the mixture is thickened and coats the back of a spoon nicely; it should hold its shape if you drag a finger through the sauce on the back of the spoon. (If you prefer to use a thermometer, the mixture should reach 180ºF.) Whisk in the honey and vanilla until smooth and combined.

Strain the milk mixture through a fine-mesh sieve into a chilled bowl to remove any cooked egg pieces. Stir the mixture to release heat, then once warm, transfer to the refrigerator and chill until completely cold, about 2 hours.

Pour the chilled milk mixture into the frozen ice cream maker bowl and churn into ice cream according to the manufacturer's instructions. Serve immediately, or transfer to a 9 x 5-inch loaf pan, cover, and store in the freezer for up to 2 weeks. If it's too hard to scoop, let it stand at room temperature for 15 to 20 minutes to soften before serving.

PISTACHIO BRITTLE

MAKES 8 OUNCES

For me, nut brittle was always a Christmastime treat, but this crunchy sundae topping changed my stance. I'm voting for brittle year-round, especially on Juneteenth. Make extra for late-night snacking.

4 tablespoons (½ stick) unsalted butter, cubed, plus 1 tablespoon for greasing

½ cup sugar

¼ cup light corn syrup

2 tablespoons water

½ cup salted shelled pistachios

¼ teaspoon baking soda

Grease a 9 x 13-inch metal baking pan with 1 tablespoon of butter.

In a medium saucepan, combine the sugar, corn syrup, and water and heat over medium heat, stirring with a rubber spatula, for 8 to 10 minutes, until the mixture comes to a boil. Add the remaining 4 tablespoons of butter to the boiling mixture one cube at a time and swirl the pan, without stirring, until all the butter is melted. Cook, swirling the pan frequently, for 15 to 20 minutes more, until a candy thermometer reaches 280ºF. The caramel will start to bubble and change from white to light brown, with the bubbles increasing in size.

Add the pistachios and cook, stirring continuously, for another 10 to 12 minutes, until a candy thermometer reaches 305ºF. If a bit of the melted mixture forms a hard strand of candy when dropped into a cup of ice water, it's done.

Remove the saucepan from the heat and carefully stir in the baking soda. Immediately transfer the hot mixture to the buttered pan. Use a spatula to level the brittle and tap the pan gently on the counter to get rid of any bubbles. Allow to cool and harden completely.

Once cool, break into small pieces. Store in an airtight container at room temperature for up to several weeks.

CORN ICE CREAM SANDWICHES

MAKES 12

Tubs of Neapolitan ice cream and vanilla ice cream sandwiches get plenty of freezer real estate in the supermarket, but to find the most interesting, compelling ice cream varieties, you have to brave the cold of the open freezer door and root around. Corn ice cream is one of those seldom seen hidden treasures that make the hunt worth it. Jeni's and La Newyorkina both sell corn ice cream as a seasonal, limited flavor. They make a good substitute here if you'd like to skip the step of making your own. But you won't want to depend on others for your supply of this treat. Buy corn during the summer months, when it's at its sweet peak, and make two batches of ice cream. Come February, you'll thank me as you dig into the second one. If you do choose to go with a store-bought variety, let it soften before scooping and sandwiching it between the cookies. Ice cream or solo—you choose. Naked, these lacy oatmeal cookies make sense if you want to save your coveted corn ice cream for an after-work binge—your guests will *ooh* and *ahh* you still.

CORN ICE CREAM (MAKES 1 QUART):

5 large egg yolks

Kernels from 3 ears fresh sweet corn (reserve the cobs), or 2½ cups thawed frozen corn kernels

6 tablespoons sour cream

1¾ cups heavy cream

½ cup granulated sugar

½ teaspoon coarse salt

2 teaspoons vanilla extract

CORN COOKIES
(MAKES 24 COOKIES):

1 cup (2 sticks) unsalted butter, melted, plus more for greasing

1 cup packed dark brown sugar

1 large egg, lightly beaten

2 teaspoons vanilla extract

¼ cup unsulfured molasses

1½ cups all-purpose flour

1 teaspoon baking soda

1 teaspoon ground allspice

1½ teaspoons ground ginger

1 teaspoon ground star anise

¾ teaspoon sea salt

1½ cups rolled oats

½ cup plus 1 tablespoon fresh corn kernels

2 tablespoons granulated sugar

Special equipment: ice cream maker

continued on page 188

Corn Ice Cream Sandwiches, *continued*

FOR THE CORN ICE CREAM: If using an ice cream maker with a freezer bowl, it'll need to be frozen for at least 12 hours before making the ice cream.

In a medium bowl, whisk the egg yolks until smooth. Mince or pulse the corn kernels a few times in a food processor.

Combine the sour cream, heavy cream, sugar, and salt in a medium saucepan over medium-high heat. Whisk to dissolve the sugar.

Add the corn. Consistently whisk the cream mixture and watch carefully; you don't want this mixture to boil. If you notice rapid bubbles, reduce the heat. Heat until the sugar dissolves, 2 to 3 minutes. Reduce the heat to medium-low.

Next, temper the egg yolks by spooning about a cup of the cream mixture into the bowl of yolks while constantly whisking. When the mixture is combined, pour the egg yolk mixture into the saucepan with the remaining cream mixture. Continue to whisk and heat the mixture until thickened; it should coat the back of a spoon nicely and hold its shape if you drag a finger through the sauce on the back of the spoon. Additionally, if you prefer to use a thermometer, the mixture should reach 180ºF. Add the vanilla and stir to combine.

Strain the milk mixture through a fine-mesh sieve into a chilled bowl to remove any cooked egg pieces. Press the corn in the sieve to release as much liquid as possible, then discard the corn. Stir the mixture to release heat, then once warm, add the reserved corn cobs and transfer to the refrigerator and chill until completely cold, about 2 hours.

Once chilled, scrape the corn cobs using the back of a knife to "milk" them.

Pour the cream mixture into the frozen ice cream bowl and make the ice cream according to manufacturer's instructions. Serve immediately or transfer to a 9 x 5-inch loaf pan and store, covered in the freezer. (The ice cream can be stored in the freezer for up to 2 weeks.)

FOR THE CORN COOKIES: Preheat the oven to 350ºF. Line two baking sheets with parchment paper.

In a large bowl, mix the melted butter and brown sugar until combined. Add the egg, vanilla, and molasses and stir again until smooth.

continued on page 190

Add the flour, baking soda, allspice, ginger, star anise, and salt and stir again to combine using a rubber spatula. Last, fold in the oats and the ½ cup of the corn kernels.

Using a 1-inch cookie scoop, place the cookie dough about 2 inches apart from each other on the prepared baking sheets.

Place the granulated sugar on a plate. Dip the bottom of a water glass in the sugar and stamp the cookies to ¼-inch thickness using the bottom of the glass. Repeat with the remaining dough balls.

Press 4 or 5 corn kernels lightly into the top of each cookie. Bake for 10 to 12 minutes, until golden and the edges are crisp. Place the baking sheets on wire baking racks to cool for 10 minutes. Then remove the cookies from the baking sheets to the racks to cool completely.

TO ASSEMBLE THE ICE CREAM SANDWICHES: If the ice cream is too hard, allow it to sit out at room temperature for 15 to 20 minutes before scooping. Place a scoop of corn ice cream on the underside of a corn cookie. Press another cookie on top of the ice cream to make a sandwich. Wrap in plastic wrap and freeze until ready to serve.

CAKE! CAKE! CAKE!

(AND A COUPLE OF PIES)

CAKE! CAKE! CAKE!

(AND A COUPLE OF PIES)

In the decades leading up to the Civil War, the fine food of the plantations would not have been possible without the creativity, hard work, and skill of enslaved cooks who cracked coconuts, caramelized sugar, sifted flour, ground sugar, and whipped eggs, without the modern conveniences we have today. —Anne Byrn, *American Cake*

It's too easy for people to say things like "working like a slave." It's as if we are so far away from actual slavery that we can allude to it casually. My almost one-hundred-year-old great-uncle remembers the mechanisms of sharecropping, when Black Americans worked for no or low wages—a vestige of the American slave system. Sometimes, when I'm in my kitchen preparing pound cake for a Fourth of July celebration, I imagine what it would have been like for my ancestors, literally slaving to prepare a strawberry pie that would never touch their lips. I'm reminded that Juneteenth didn't symbolize the end of work; it signified the beginning of working for yourself, working for your loved ones rather than for someone else's loved ones (without pay). That thought can make me smile while I'm peeling that peach for cobbler.

The term "cakewalk" has two definitions. First, the cakewalk was a dance performed by enslaved Black people for their plantation owners. Nineteenth-century Black Americans dressed up—the women in billowing lace-edged gowns and the men in tuxedos and high hats. A towering dessert—that they had made—propped on a table. This is the depiction of the cakewalk from period postcard artwork. Later, the word "cakewalk" became slang for a simple task. We talk about a "cakewalk" too quickly regarding the second definition without acknowledging the first. In an article about the cakewalk on NPR's *Code Switch* blog, Lakshmi Gandhi writes, "The uniquely American dance was first known as the 'prize walk'; the prize was an elaborately decorated cake. Hence, 'prize walk' is the original source for the phrases 'takes the cake' and 'cakewalk.'" To "take the cake" in a competition among serious dancers would not have been easy.

Entertaining white spectators and baking fruit pies and layered cakes for individuals who believed you didn't have the intellectual capacity to measure flour or weigh butter—it is enough to make one never want to return to the hearth. And yet we still head to our countertops to make desserts that celebrate life. This painful history aside, cakes are still the cornerstones of the Juneteenth table. What would celebrations be without cake? Honey whispering in vanilla and syrup dancing in batter, you want your guests to leave with a sweet taste in their mouths.

PEACH CRUMBLE PIE BARS

MAKES ONE 8-INCH PAN, SERVES 12

On special occasions, like the last day of Vacation Bible School, always held in the summertime, my favorite cousins, Tom and Bonnie Gartrell—who were more like an aunt and uncle to me—would make sandy-colored bars or blondies. They'd serve these to all the attendees. For this recipe, I riff off the summer fruit and classic peach cobbler and my cousin's flavor notes.

CRUMBLE TOPPING:

2 tablespoons packed dark brown sugar

2 tablespoons granulated sugar

¼ teaspoon ground cinnamon

½ teaspoon freshly ground mace

2 tablespoons unsalted butter, melted

¼ cup all-purpose flour

¼ teaspoon sea salt

PEACHES:

½ cup (1 stick) unsalted butter, melted

¼ cup packed dark brown sugar

½ cup granulated sugar

1 large egg

2 teaspoons vanilla extract

1¼ cups all-purpose flour

¼ teaspoon sea salt

1 cup peeled sliced ripe peaches (sliced ¼ inch thick) or thawed frozen peach slices (see Note)

Preheat the oven to 350°F. Line an 8-inch square baking pan with parchment paper, letting some hang over the sides to act as handles.

FOR THE CRUMBLE TOPPING: In a medium bowl, combine the dark brown sugar, granulated sugar, cinnamon, mace, melted butter, flour, and salt. Stir

continued on page 200

Peach Crumble Pie Bars, *continued*

using a wooden spoon until well combined (use your hands if needed); the mixture should form small clumps. Set aside.

FOR THE PEACHES: In a medium bowl, combine the melted butter, dark brown sugar, and granulated sugar. Add the egg and vanilla extract and whisk to combine. Add the flour and salt and mix until a smooth, soft dough forms. Press the dough evenly over the bottom of the prepared baking pan. Use an offset spatula to smooth and spread the dough.

Lay the peaches gently over the dough in even rows. Sprinkle the crumble topping over the peaches and bake for 30 to 35 minutes, until a toothpick inserted into the center comes out clean. The edges of the bars should be golden and the crumble lightly browned.

Allow to cool for 10 minutes in the pan before removing (using the overhanging parchment as handles) and slicing into squares. Store leftover bars in an airtight container or wrapped in plastic wrap at room temperature for up to 3 days.

NOTE: If using frozen peaches (or strawberries, blueberries, blackberries for recipes in this chapter), defrost them in a small bowl and drain off any excess liquid, then toss with 1 tablespoon brown sugar and set them aside until you need them.

PEACH CRUMB CAKE

MAKES ONE 8-INCH PAN, SERVES 12

Remember the peach crumble pie bars on page 199? This is a variation of that flavor combination. I love eating cake for breakfast. I did that at the Grey Market in Savannah where James Beard Award–winning chef Mashama Bailey is at the helm. Crumb cake is perfect after grits and fresh-pressed juice. Make this the morning of your Juneteenth party and pray you have leftovers to wake up to the following day.

1 tablespoon unsalted butter, at room temperature, for greasing

CRUMBLE TOPPING:

6 tablespoons packed dark brown sugar

3 tablespoons granulated sugar

¾ teaspoon ground cinnamon

1½ teaspoons freshly ground mace

6 tablespoons unsalted butter, melted

¾ cup all-purpose flour

PEACH CAKE:

½ cup (1 stick) unsalted butter, at room temperature

1 cup granulated sugar

2 large eggs

½ cup whole milk

½ cup sour cream

½ cup chopped peeled peaches (chopped ¼ inch thick)

2 cups all-purpose flour

¼ teaspoon kosher salt

1¼ teaspoons baking powder

Preheat the oven to 375ºF. Grease an 8-inch square baking pan with the butter.

FOR THE CRUMBLE TOPPING: In a medium bowl, combine the brown sugar, granulated sugar, cinnamon, mace, butter, and flour in a medium bowl. Mix to

continued on page 202

Peach Crumb Cake, *continued*

combine using a wooden spoon, stirring until small crumbles form (feel free to use your hands for this as well!). Set aside.

FOR THE PEACH CAKE: In the bowl of a stand mixer fitted with the paddle attachment or in a medium bowl using a handheld mixer, cream the butter and sugar until light and fluffy on medium speed for 3 minutes.

Add the eggs, one at a time, mixing just until each is incorporated. Add the milk, sour cream, and the chopped peaches and mix again for 1 to 2 minutes, until combined.

Add the flour in batches with the salt and baking powder and continue to mix on medium-low speed until a smooth batter forms.

Transfer the batter to the prepared baking pan and evenly spread using a spatula. Sprinkle the crumble on top and add a single layer of peach slices.

Bake for 50 to 60 minutes, until a cake tester inserted into the center comes out clean. Allow to cool in the pan for 15 minutes before slicing and serving. Store leftover cake in an airtight container or wrapped in plastic wrap at room temperature for up to 3 days.

STRAWBERRY HAND PIES

MAKES TEN 5-INCH HAND PIES

When I hear a friend recount watching her nana's work-worn and weathered hands making fried fruit pies, I want to know everything. Does her nana use vegetable shortening for the crust? Does she prefer preserved or fresh stone fruit for the filling? Does she fry, or bake, her pies? It's more detail than any friend can recall. These things, which seem so essential to me, aren't important to everyone. If you're reading this, I hope you'll pay attention next time, and report back.

Most often, I fry my hand pies, but I've opted to use the oven method here. You still get plenty of crunchy richness from the buttery crust and summer fruit magic from the filling.

GOAT CHEESE FROSTING:

3 ounces goat cheese, at room temperature

1 tablespoon unsalted butter, at room temperature

1½ cups confectioners' sugar

¾ teaspoon vanilla extract

DOUGH:

2½ cups plus 2 tablespoons all-purpose flour, plus more for dusting

2 teaspoons granulated sugar

1 teaspoon kosher salt

1 teaspoon cracked black pepper

1 cup (2 sticks) unsalted butter, cut into ½-inch cubes and chilled

¾ cup ice water

STRAWBERRY FILLING:

12 ounces fresh strawberries, hulled and finely chopped

1 to 2 tablespoons loosely packed dark brown sugar, depending on how sweet your berries are

¾ teaspoon cornstarch

½ teaspoon grapefruit zest

1 teaspoon fresh grapefruit juice

¼ teaspoon grated fresh ginger

¼ teaspoon vanilla extract

⅛ teaspoon kosher salt

1 large egg, beaten with 1 tablespoon water, for the egg wash

FOR THE GOAT CHEESE FROSTING: Place the goat cheese and butter in the bowl of a stand mixer fitted with the paddle attachment, or in a medium bowl using a handheld mixer. Beat on medium speed until smooth, 1 to 2 minutes, scraping down the sides as needed to eliminate lumps.

continued on page 204

Strawberry Hand Pies, *continued*

Working ½ cup at a time, add in the confectioners' sugar. Stir in the vanilla. Transfer to a plastic container and store in the refrigerator for up to 1 week.

FOR THE DOUGH: Preheat oven to 350ºF. Line a baking sheet with parchment paper. Set aside. Place a pastry blender or two butter knives in the freezer.

In a large bowl, whisk together the flour, sugar, salt, and pepper. Using a pastry blender, cut the butter into the flour mixture until the largest pieces of butter are the size of small peas.

Sprinkle the ice water over the dough, a tablespoon at a time, stirring and scooping the dough with your hands as you go to incorporate the water, until the dough just begins to adhere and you can gather it into an imperfect ball (you may not need all the water).

Transfer the dough to a piece of plastic wrap and press into a disc. Wrap tightly and place in the fridge for 30 minutes.

FOR THE STRAWBERRY FILLING: Meanwhile, in a medium bowl, combine the strawberries, brown sugar, cornstarch, grapefruit zest and juice, ginger, vanilla, and salt. Allow to macerate while the pie dough chills for 30 minutes.

Lightly dust a large work surface, a rolling pin, and the dough with flour. Roll the chilled dough into an ⅛-inch-thick rectangle.

From that, cut 5-inch diameter circles. Reroll scraps and chill again for 10 minutes to make more.

Fill each pie crust with 1 heaping tablespoon of the strawberry filling. Fold over the dough into a half moon shape and crimp closed with the prongs of a fork. Chill the pies in the fridge until ready to bake.

Brush the tops of the pies with the egg wash and prick with a fork twice to create vents. Bake for 30 to 35 minutes, until golden brown. Remove the pies from the oven and allow to cool completely. Once cooled, spread the goat cheese frosting over each pie before serving. Store leftover pies in an airtight container or wrapped in plastic wrap at room temperature for up to 3 days.

TIP: If you plan to go on a baking spree, buy a thermometer for your oven. Believe it or not, the temperature on the dial is often a little bit off and can mess with baking times.

MAKE IT SHAKE

A pie milkshake is a treat that is a grand gesture. It's the colorful straw for sure. The hand-pie crust gives the shake a fullness, but everything is balanced with the honey vanilla ice cream and milk. In a blender, combine 1 hand pie, 2 scoops of ice cream, and ⅓ cup whole milk (depending on your desired texture, you might want to add a bit more milk). Pour into two collins-like glasses. Sprinkle with crushed dried strawberries and serve.

STRAWBERRY & BLACK PEPPER SLAB PIE

MAKES ONE 14×12 SLAB, TO SERVE 8 TO 10

I developed a similar recipe for the first story I wrote about red foods of Juneteenth for the *New York Times* Food section. The crust is the difference; I'm using puff pastry here. It's a great substitute for those times when you don't have the time or energy to make a piecrust from scratch. I always keep extra cartons of frozen puff pastry around for impromptu dinner parties.

The berries might not be a surprise like the cracked pepper here. I love cracked pepper and am constantly trying different sources and varieties of peppercorns. Pepper works surprisingly well when paired with sweet fruit.

BERRY FILLING:

2 cups fresh strawberries, small berries halved and larger berries, hulled and quartered (see page 200)

4 cups blackberries

5 tablespoons sugar

3 tablespoons cornstarch

1 tablespoon fresh orange juice

¼ teaspoon sea salt

½ teaspoon vanilla extract

½ teaspoon freshly cracked black pepper

PIECRUST:

All-purpose flour, for dusting

2 (17.3-ounce) sheets frozen puff pastry, thawed

1 large egg, beaten with 1 tablespoon water, for the egg wash

1½ teaspoons sugar

FOR THE BERRY FILLING: In a large saucepan, combine the strawberries, blackberries, sugar, cornstarch, orange juice, salt, vanilla, and pepper and bring to a simmer over medium-low heat. Simmer, stirring occasionally, for about

continued on page 208

10 minutes, or until the berries have broken down a little but still have some shape. Remove from the heat and allow to cool completely.

FOR THE PIECRUST: Preheat the oven to 400ºF. Line a baking sheet with parchment paper.

On a surface lightly dusted with flour, roll out one sheet of the puff pastry to a 14 x 12-inch rectangle. Place it on the prepared baking sheet. Roll out the second sheet of puff pastry to the same size and cut out six to eight 1-inch circles using a biscuit cutter.

Spread the cooled fruit mixture over the large rectangle of puff pastry, leaving a 1-inch border. Brush the border with the egg wash. Top with the sheet of puff pastry with the holes. Pinch the edges of the pastry together and crimp using the prongs of a fork to seal.

Brush the crust with the egg wash and sprinkle with the sugar. Bake for 28 to 30 minutes, until the puff pastry is golden brown and the filling is bubbling.

Allow to cool until just warm, an hour or so, then cut into squares and serve. Store leftover pie in an airtight container or wrapped in plastic wrap at room temperature for up to 3 days.

STRAWBERRY SUMAC CAKE

MAKES ONE 9-INCH PAN, SERVES 6 TO 8

In the Mediterranean and the Middle East, cooks know the acidic tang of crimson dried powdered sumac as a kitchen staple. Sumac doesn't get a lot of love in American kitchens, even though edible sumac species grow wild throughout America and is essential in the Indigenous American kitchen. If you want to forage for the wild variety, the fall season is the time to do it, look for sumac with red berry clusters like staghorn sumac, not white (that's poison sumac). Foraging is back in style for a new generation of Black Americans. "Whether they're herbalists, Great Migration grandbabies in search of Southern roots, shoppers slashing their food budgets, the only Black kids who went to 4-H camp back in the day, or home cooks who want to dazzle guests with a backyard-berry crostata," Dr. Cynthia Greenlee wrote in a July 2021 *New York Times* article titled "How Black Foragers Find Freedom in the Natural World," they are going "shopping" in the woods.

STRAWBERRIES:

1 cup chopped hulled fresh strawberries (1-inch dice), plus 1 cup strawberries, halved

1 teaspoon ground sumac

1 teaspoon sugar

½ teaspoon almond extract

CAKE:

1 cup plus 1 tablespoon "everyday" olive oil

2 cups all-purpose flour

1 cup stone ground yellow cornmeal

½ teaspoon kosher salt

½ teaspoon baking soda

½ teaspoon baking powder

3 large eggs

1 cup plus 2 tablespoons sugar

½ cup half-and-half

¼ teaspoon ground sumac

FOR THE STRAWBERRIES: Combine the diced strawberries, sumac, sugar, and almond extract in a small bowl and set aside to macerate while you're preparing the cake.

FOR THE CAKE: Preheat the oven to 350ºF. Grease a 9-inch round cake pan or springform pan with 1 tablespoon olive oil.

continued on page 212

Strawberry Sumac Cake, *continued*

In a large bowl, whisk together the all-purpose flour, cornmeal, salt, baking soda, and baking powder to combine. Set aside.

In the bowl of a stand mixer fitted with the whisk attachment or in a medium bowl using a handheld mixer, beat the eggs and 1 cup sugar on medium-high speed until very pale and light yellow in color, about 3 minutes. The mixture should thicken and make ribbons that slowly lose their shape when they fall off the whisk attachment. With the mixer on high speed, slowly add the remaining 1 cup olive oil and beat until everything is combined and the mixture is thickened further.

Reduce the speed to medium-low and slowly begin adding the dry ingredients in three additions, adding the half-and-half halfway through. Mix until just combined.

Remove the bowl from the stand mixer and fold in the diced strawberries and their liquid. Pour the batter into the prepared pan, smoothing the top with a spatula. Arrange the halved strawberries on the top. Bake for 40 to 50 minutes, until the cake is golden brown and a toothpick inserted into the center comes out clean.

In a small bowl, mix the remaining 2 tablespoons sugar with the sumac. Sprinkle the cake with the sumac sugar while still slightly warm.

Allow the cake to cool in the pan on a wire rack for 20 minutes. Turn the cake out of the pan onto the rack or release the springform ring and remove it. Let cool completely before serving. Store leftover cake in an airtight container or wrapped in plastic wrap at room temperature for up to 4 days.

RADISH & GINGER POUND CAKE

MAKES ONE 10-INCH BUNDT CAKE, SERVES 10 TO 12

This is not church lady pound cake with flavors powered by lemon and butter and vanilla extract. Nothing against those old recipes. They will always have a home in my kitchen. But sometimes I like to play with tradition, and here's a tasty tune-up to that old classic. The ginger root and radish play well together, the ginger adding spice and the radish adding a satisfying chew. The moistness and texture are the closest characteristics to old-school Bundt cake. The proof of perfection is in the cream.

CAKE:

1 cup (2 sticks) unsalted butter, plus 1 tablespoon for greasing

2½ cups all-purpose flour, plus 2 tablespoons for dusting

1 cup (8-ounce package) cream cheese

2½ cups granulated sugar

6 large eggs

1 teaspoon ground ginger

½ teaspoon kosher salt

½ teaspoon dried lemon peel or fresh lemon zest

⅓ cup grated red radish

WHIPPED RADISH AND GINGER CREAM:

1 cup heavy cream, chilled

2 teaspoons packed light brown sugar

2 teaspoons grated red radish

1 teaspoon finely grated fresh ginger (grated on a Microplane)

Confectioners' sugar, for dusting

FOR THE CAKE: Preheat the oven to 350°F with a rack in the middle of the oven. Grease a 10-inch (10-cup) Bundt pan with 1 tablespoon butter and dust with 2 tablespoons flour, shaking out any excess.

continued on page 215

Radish & Ginger Pound Cake, *continued*

In the bowl of a stand mixer fitted with the paddle attachment or in a large bowl using a handheld mixer, beat the butter, cream cheese, and granulated sugar on medium-high speed until smooth and fluffy, 2 to 3 minutes. Add the eggs one at a time, mixing on medium-low speed until each is just incorporated before adding the next. To provide better streaks (the moist crumb spots in a perfectly done cake), please do not overmix here or while adding the eggs and flour.

With the mixer on low speed, add the remaining 2½ cups flour in three batches, allowing the mixer to incorporate the flour. Scrape down the sides of the bowl with a spatula as necessary. Add the ginger, salt, lemon peel, and grated radish and mix again until just combined.

Pour the batter into the prepared pan and smooth the top. Bake for about 1 hour 30 minutes, or until golden brown and a toothpick inserted into the center comes out clean. Remove from the oven and allow to cool in the pan on a wire rack for 20 minutes. Remove the cake from the pan and allow to cool completely on the rack.

FOR THE WHIPPED RADISH AND GINGER CREAM: In the clean bowl of a stand mixer fitted with the whisk attachment or in a large bowl using a handheld mixer, beat the cream and brown sugar on medium-high speed until soft peaks form. Remove the bowl from the stand mixer and gently fold in the grated radish and ginger by hand.

Dust the top of the cake with confectioners' sugar. Slice and serve, topping each slice with a dollop of the whipped radish and ginger cream. Store leftover cake in an airtight container or wrapped in plastic wrap at room temperature for up to 4 days.

FLORIDA PUNCH BOWL CAKE

SERVES 12

The city of St. Petersburg is so close, but far away, and I'm all ears when my dear friend Reginald Dye talks about his mother Georgetta's childhood in Florida, where orange mango trees dotted the front yard. A punch bowl cake is America's version of a trifle, that layered English dessert (with its own designated bowl). I opt out of the pudding for my explosion of edible colors.

UNSWEETENED CREAM:

1 quart chilled heavy cream

Radish & Ginger Pound Cake (page 213), cooled and then cubed

¾ cup (about 6 ounces) lemon marmalade

1 cup coconut flakes

1 cup orange juice

4 cups pineapple, cubed (from about 1 pineapple)

4 cups mango, thinly sliced lengthwise (from about 4 mangos)

3 cups kiwi, thinly sliced lengthwise (from about 10 kiwis)

Edible flowers (optional)

MERINGUE TOPPING (OPTIONAL):

3 large egg whites, at room temperature

¼ teaspoon cream of tartar

½ teaspoon vanilla extract

¾ cup granulated sugar

Optional equipment: kitchen torch

FOR THE WHIPPED CREAM: Make the whipped cream according to the instructions on page 174; hold the sugar. Set aside in the fridge.

Organize your "assembly" line and remove your whipped cream from the fridge. In a large glass punch bowl, layer a third of the ingredients as follows: cake, marmalade, coconut flakes, orange juice, pineapple, mango, kiwi, then whipped cream. Repeat twice more, for a total of three layers. Store leftovers in an airtight container in the refrigerator for a few days.

Swirl the meringue topping on top of the cake. Toast with a kitchen torch. Also, add edible flowers: nasturtium, pansies, lavender, violet, marigold, and/or sweet pea.

FOR THE MERINGUE TOPPING: In the bowl of a stand mixer fitted with the whisk attachment or in a medium bowl using a handheld mixer, beat the egg whites on low speed until they begin to foam, about 2 minutes. Add the cream of tartar, vanilla, and one-third of the sugar and beat on medium speed until the whites become opaque, another 2 minutes or so.

Add another third of the sugar and beat on medium-high speed for 2 minutes. Add the remaining sugar and beat on medium-high speed until the whites double in size and reach firm peaks. You'll know you have firm peaks when you can lift the whisk out of the bowl and the meringue stands up without deflating.

KAYLAH'S TEA CAKES

MAKES 4 DOZEN

If you do an internet search for "tea cakes," you'll get a wide variety of things, many of which I wouldn't call tea cakes. There are tea cakes with icing, tea cakes that are really muffins, tea cakes with a thick cakelike profile like madeleines. The tea cakes Chef Kaylah Thomas brought to my 2019 Juneteenth terrace party were the first I remember eating: more cookie than cake, subtly spiced, and not too sweet. American tea cakes are most associated with the enslaved cook and the African American dessert canon. Toni Tipton-Martin writes in *Jubilee*, "They show up in black cookbooks—a lot."

½ cup (1 stick) unsalted butter

½ cup vegetable shortening, or
17 tablespoons unsalted butter

1 cup granulated sugar

2 large eggs

2¾ cups all-purpose flour

1 teaspoon baking soda

2 teaspoons cream of tartar

½ teaspoon kosher salt

1 teaspoon ground allspice

¼ teaspoon ground ginger

In the bowl of a stand mixer fitted with the paddle attachment or in a large bowl using a handheld mixer, cream the butter, shortening, and sugar on medium-high speed until smooth, about 2 minutes. Add the eggs and beat until just combined.

Add half the flour and beat to incorporate, then add the remaining flour, the baking soda, cream of tartar, salt, allspice, and ginger and beat until combined and smooth. Wrap the dough in plastic wrap and refrigerate until firm, 30 minutes to 1 hour.

When ready to bake, preheat the oven to 350ºF. Line two baking sheets with parchment paper.

Using a tablespoon measure, scoop the dough into rounds and place them on the prepared baking sheets, spacing them 2 inches apart from each other. (If not all the tea cakes fit on the baking sheets at once, you can bake them in batches.) Bake for 7 to 9 minutes, until golden brown. Allow to cool on the baking sheets for 10 minutes, then transfer to a wire rack and allow to cool completely.

Store the tea cakes in an airtight container at room temperature for up to 5 days.

MOSCATO POUND CAKE

MAKES ONE 10-INCH BUNDT CAKE, SERVES 10 TO 12

I'd been pondering the phenomenon of African Americans consuming moscato throughout a meal or before dinner—and opting out of drinking it as a traditional dessert wine. Moscato might be Italian in origin, but it has become such a standard beverage for Black Americans that you'd be wise to keep a bottle on hand for unexpected company. This recipe combines the yin and the yang of the old and the new that I also like. Most folks grew up on pound cake but have only recently acquired a taste for moscato. Why not put them together? It seemed to me that putting moscato in the cake itself would be the perfect way to use a sparkling wine that's sweet enough to be a dessert in its own right.

CAKE:

2 cups (4 sticks) unsalted butter, at room temperature, plus additional for greasing

4 cups all-purpose flour, plus additional for dusting

¾ cup (6 ounces) Moscato d'Asti

2 teaspoons fresh lemon juice

1 teaspoon vanilla extract

3 cups granulated sugar

1 teaspoon fine sea salt

6 large eggs, at room temperature

GRAPE GLAZE:

½ cup dehydrated seedless red grape slices (see Tip, page 60)

1 cup confectioners' sugar

2 tablespoons plus 1½ teaspoons (1¼ ounces) Moscato d'Asti or fresh lime juice

¼ teaspoon fine sea salt

FOR THE CAKE: Preheat the oven to 300°F. Grease a 10-inch (10-cup) Bundt pan with butter and dust it with flour, shaking out any excess.

In a small bowl, combine the Moscato, lemon juice, and vanilla. Set aside.

In the bowl of a stand mixer fitted with the paddle attachment or in a medium bowl using a handheld mixer, beat the butter on medium speed until pale yellow and smooth, about 5 minutes. With the mixer running, gradually add

continued on page 220

the sugar and salt and beat until light and fluffy, about 5 minutes, stopping occasionally to scrape down the sides of the bowl. Add the eggs one at a time, beating well after each addition. With the mixer running on low speed, add the flour in batches, alternating with the moscato mixture, and mix until just combined.

Scrape the batter into the prepared Bundt pan and smooth the top. Bake for 1 hour 40 minutes to 1 hour 50 minutes, until a toothpick inserted into the center comes out clean. Allow the cake to cool in the pan on a wire rack for 15 minutes. Then turn the cake out of the pan and set it on the rack to cool completely, about 2 hours.

FOR THE GRAPE GLAZE: Place the dehydrated grape slices and ¼ cup of the confectioners' sugar in a spice grinder or mini food processor and pulse until a fine powder forms, about 30 seconds. Sift the powder through a fine-mesh sieve into a small bowl, discarding any clumps.

Add 2 tablespoons of the moscato, the salt, and the remaining ¾ cup confectioners' sugar and combine. Add the remaining 1½ teaspoons moscato, ½ teaspoon at a time, until the glaze reaches the desired consistency. Drizzle the glaze evenly over the cake and allow to set for 15 minutes before serving.

Store the cake in an airtight container in the refrigerator for up to 4 days.

BLUEBERRY & BEEF PUFF PIES

MAKES TWELVE TO FOURTEEN 5-INCH PIES

Americans don't usually mix fruit and meat. We've taken a lot of traditions from the British, but mincemeat pie—which commonly combines a mixture of dried fruit, rum or brandy, beef, and beef suet—is not one of them. Mincemeat pie, or at least its inspiration, is not even British. It's based on flavors combining fruit and meat, sweet and savory, that British Crusaders tasted in the Middle East as early as the thirteenth century. Perhaps the problem is that mincemeat pie has many of the same ingredients as those infamously bad Christmas fruitcakes, plus meat, which might seem out of place to the American palate. The blueberries and honey here give a hint of sweetness to the dish, but it tastes more like a beef pie than a blueberry one. If possible, use fresh berries to avoid the extra step of defrosting frozen blueberries. The filling can be wrapped in a corn tortilla or Bibb lettuce instead of puff pastry—perfect for a Juneteenth picnic. Every picnic needs easy "wrap up in a napkin" foods like this one.

½ tablespoon "everyday" olive oil

8 ounces ground beef

½ canned chipotle pepper in adobo sauce, minced

1 teaspoon kosher salt

½ cup plus 2 tablespoons fresh blueberries

2 scallions, thinly sliced (heaping ¼ cup)

1 tablespoon honey

¼ cup grated Pecorino Romano cheese

All-purpose flour, for dusting

2 (17.3-ounce) sheets frozen puff pastry, thawed

1 large egg, beaten

½ teaspoon chili powder

Flaky sea salt, for garnish

1 large egg, beaten with 1 tablespoon water, for the egg wash

In a large skillet, heat the olive oil over medium-high heat. When the oil is shimmering, add the ground beef and cook, undisturbed, for 2 to 3 minutes, until browned on the bottom. Using a wooden spoon, break up the beef and cook until all the beef is browned, 6 to 8 minutes more. Season the beef with the chipotle pepper and salt during the last minute of cooking.

Add the blueberries and scallions and cook until the blueberries are softened and blistered, 8 to 10 minutes.

Remove the beef mixture from the heat and stir in the honey and cheese. Transfer to a bowl and allow to cool for 5 minutes, then refrigerate for 15 minutes to cool further.

Meanwhile, preheat the oven to 400ºF. Line two baking sheets with parchment paper.

On a surface lightly dusted with flour, roll the puff pastry slightly so no creases remain. Cut out 5-inch rounds from the puff pastry using a bowl or round biscuit cutter. Gather the pastry scraps, roll them out, and cut additional rounds, to make 12 to 14 total. Fill each round of puff pastry with 1 tablespoon of the beef mixture, leaving a ½-inch or so border of puff pastry.

Brush the exposed pastry border with some of the egg wash. Fold the dough over the filling to make a half-moon and crimp the edges using the prongs of a fork to seal. Brush the tops of the pies with the egg and sprinkle with the chili powder and some flaky salt.

Place the pies ½ inch apart on the prepared baking sheets and bake for 12 to 14 minutes, until golden brown. Allow to cool for 5 minutes before serving. Store leftover pies in an airtight container or wrapped in plastic wrap in the refrigerator for up to a couple of days.

DEVIL'S FOOD ICEBOX CAKE

MAKES ONE 9 X 5-INCH LOAF CAKE, SERVES 8 TO 10

When you think of red foods and Black food traditions, red velvet cake might come to mind, but red food coloring was a luxury until the late 1930s and cream cheese frosting was introduced to the masses in the 1940s. In fact, it was probably a fluffy dark brown cake made with chocolate or cocoa that showed up at Black celebrations. I'm throwing it back to the original color with this dessert.

Juneteenth coincides with summer heat. It's a time when a lot of us are trying to spend as little time in the kitchen as possible. This dessert requires minimal baking and so is perfect for the dog days of June. But if you're up for it, I think making your wafers from scratch is very rewarding. Often when we buy a prepackaged, ready-made ingredient, we infer that we could never make it at home because we don't have a big cookie factory with teams of workers. But everything they make at a dessert factory started with one or two people in a research kitchen doing things that you could do at home.

1½ (8-ounce) packages cream cheese, at room temperature

1½ cups confectioners' sugar

2 tablespoons unsweetened cocoa powder

2 cups heavy cream

24 to 36 chocolate wafers, homemade (recipe follows) or store-bought, such as Nabisco

1 cup pecans, chopped

CHOCOLATE WAFERS
(MAKES 36):

1½ cups all-purpose flour

½ cup unsweetened cocoa powder

½ teaspoon fine sea salt

½ teaspoon baking powder

½ cup (1 stick) unsalted butter, at room temperature

¾ cup granulated sugar

continued on page 226

Devil's Food Icebox Cake, *continued*

¼ **cup packed dark brown sugar**

1 large egg

1 tablespoon whole milk

1 teaspoon vanilla extract

FOR THE CAKE: Line a 9 x 5-inch loaf pan with plastic wrap, leaving a 6-inch overhang on both long sides to act as handles.

In the bowl of a stand mixer fitted with the paddle attachment or in a large bowl using a handheld mixer, beat the cream cheese until smooth. Add the confectioners' sugar and cocoa powder and beat until fully incorporated, light, and smooth.

Switch the paddle attachment out for the whisk attachment. Add the heavy cream to the cream cheese mixture and beat on low speed until there are no lumps, then increase the speed to medium and whip to soft peaks.

Place a single layer of chocolate wafers on the bottom of the prepared loaf pan, breaking any additional wafers in half to fill in the extra space. Spread a generous ½ cup of the chocolate whipped cream over them. Repeat this process four more times to make a total of five layers, finishing with the whipped cream.

Bring up the overhanging plastic wrap on the sides of the pan and cover the cake. Chill in the refrigerator for at least 12 hours and ideally up to 24 hours, until the wafers have softened to a cakelike texture.

When ready to serve, unwrap the cake and turn it out of the pan onto a platter. Remove the pan and plastic wrap. Gently press the pecans against the sides of the cake. Slice into 1-inch-thick pieces and serve. Store leftover cake in an airtight container or wrapped in plastic wrap in the refrigerator for up to 3 days.

FOR THE CHOCOLATE WAFERS: In a large bowl, whisk together the flour, cocoa powder, salt, and baking powder. Set aside.

In the bowl of a stand mixer fitted with the paddle attachment or in a medium bowl using a handheld mixer, cream the butter, granulated sugar, and dark brown sugar on medium-high speed until smooth and fluffy, about 3 minutes. Add the egg, milk, and vanilla and mix on low speed until just incorporated. With the mixer on low speed, add the flour mixture in 1-cup increments and mix until the flour is well combined and a soft dough forms.

Place the dough on the counter and knead it a couple of times using your hands. Roll the dough into a 2-inch-thick log and wrap in plastic wrap or parchment paper, twisting the ends to seal. Chill in the refrigerator for at least 30 minutes and up to overnight, until the dough is solid and easy to slice with a knife (this is also the point where the dough can be frozen for up to a month, if desired).

When ready to bake, preheat the oven to 350ºF and line two baking sheets with parchment paper. Slice the chilled dough crosswise into ¼-inch-thick rounds and place them 1 inch apart on the prepared baking sheets. (If you can't fit all the wafers on the baking sheets at once, you can bake them in batches.)

Bake for 8 to 10 minutes, until the wafers are set and appear dry. Allow to cool on the baking sheets for 5 minutes, then transfer to a wire rack to cool completely until crisp. Store in an airtight container at room temperature for up to 4 days.

BLACKBERRY ETON MESS

SERVES 4

Why would someone name a dish "Eton Mess" if they intended for people to eat it? That I can't answer, except to say that the mix of berries, cream, and meringue is often served without the benefit of fancy presentation. The ingredients, strewn about on a dessert plate, can look a little messy. Pavlova, the Down Under dessert that is a lot like an Eton Mess, boasts a meringue that is fluffy, carefully shaped, and filled with fruit. I've used blackberries here, but any summer fruit can be substituted. This is a perfect showcase for whatever fruit looks best in your market. Store-bought meringues are fine if you're in a time crunch.

BLACKBERRY COULIS:

1½ cups fresh blackberries

⅓ cup granulated sugar

½ cup water

1 teaspoon aromatic bitters

MERINGUES:

3 large egg whites, at room temperature

¼ teaspoon cream of tartar

½ teaspoon vanilla extract

¾ cup granulated sugar

WHIPPED CREAM:

1 cup chilled heavy cream

1 tablespoon confectioners' sugar

½ cup fresh blackberries, halved if large, for topping

FOR THE BLACKBERRY COULIS: In a small saucepan, combine the blackberries, granulated sugar, and water and bring to a boil over medium-high heat. Reduce the heat to medium-low and simmer for 5 to 7 minutes, until the sugar is dissolved. Remove from the heat and allow to cool for 5 minutes.

Transfer the mixture to a food processor or a high-speed blender. Process until smooth. Strain the coulis through a fine-mesh sieve into a heatproof plastic container. Stir in the bitters, cover, and refrigerate until chilled. (The coulis can be stored in the refrigerator for up to 5 days.)

FOR THE MERINGUES: Preheat the oven to 250ºF. Line a baking sheet with parchment paper.

In the bowl of a stand mixer fitted with the whisk attachment or in a medium bowl using a handheld mixer, beat the egg whites on low speed until they begin to foam, about 2 minutes. Add the cream of tartar, vanilla, and one-third of the sugar and beat on medium speed until the whites become opaque, another 2 minutes or so.

continued on page 230

Add another third of the sugar and beat on medium-high speed for 2 minutes. Add the remaining sugar and beat on medium-high speed until the whites double in size and reach firm peaks. You'll know you have firm peaks when you can lift the whisk out of the bowl and the meringue stands up without deflating.

Dollop four ½-cup mounds of the meringue on the prepared baking sheet using a large spoon. (Alternatively, you can spoon 32 tablespoon-size dollops of the meringue onto the baking sheet, spaced 1 inch apart.) Bake on the middle rack for 1 hour to 1 hour 20 minutes, until the meringues are hardened on the outside and lightly toasted on the bottom. They should sound hollow when tapped. Turn off the oven and use a wooden spoon to crack the door open. Leave the meringues in the oven to cool completely. (The meringues will keep in an airtight container in a cool, dry place for up to 3 days.)

FOR THE WHIPPED CREAM: In the clean bowl of a stand mixer fitted with the whisk attachment or in a large bowl using a handheld mixer, combine the heavy cream and confectioners' sugar. Beat on medium-high speed until the cream is doubled in volume and medium-stiff peaks have formed. Chill in the refrigerator until ready to serve.

When ready to serve, break each meringue into large pieces. In four dessert glasses or bowls, layer the meringue pieces, blackberry coulis, fresh blackberries, then whipped cream, and repeat until the bowl or glass is full. Serve immediately.

CHILE MARSHMALLOW PIES

MAKES TWELVE 2¾-INCH PIES

MoonPies are a quintessential Southern snack food. The pies themselves were invented in 1917. This made-from-scratch variation on the old classic is much more to my liking—not so sweet, and complete with a variety of different textures—first, the cake of the graham crackers, then the cloudlike softness of the marshmallows, the surprise pop of jalapeño chile pepper, and the rich, creamy sweetness of the chocolate. Remember to buy high-quality chocolate for enrobing the pie.

CHILE MARSHMALLOWS:

Vegetable oil spray

3 (¼-ounce) packets unflavored gelatin powder

¾ cup cold water

3 jalapeños

1 lime, juiced, about 2 tablespoons

½ teaspoon kosher salt

2 cups granulated sugar

⅔ cup light corn syrup

Confectioners' sugar, for dusting

GRAHAM CRACKERS (MAKES 24 CRACKERS):

2 cups all-purpose flour, plus more for dusting

½ cup buckwheat flour

¼ teaspoon baking soda

¼ teaspoon kosher salt

½ cup (1 stick) unsalted butter, at room temperature

½ cup granulated sugar

½ cup packed light brown sugar

½ cup water

12 ounces dark chocolate, chopped and divided, for dipping

Special equipment: 2¾-inch (7mm) round cutter

FOR THE CHILE MARSHMALLOWS: Grease a 9 x 13-inch baking sheet with vegetable oil spray.

In the bowl of a stand mixer fitted with the whisk attachment or in a large bowl using a handheld mixer, combine the gelatin with ½ cup of the cold water. Set the gelatin mixture aside to bloom for 10 minutes.

continued on page 234

Chile Marshmallow Pie, *continued*

Blister the jalapeños for 2 to 3 minutes in a cast-iron pan on high heat or directly on a gas burner using tongs until slightly softened and burnt all over. Let the peppers cool. Remove the stems and seeds. Mince well. Mix the peppers with the lime juice in a nonreactive bowl. Add to the gelatin mixture.

Meanwhile, in a small saucepan, combine the remaining ¼ cup cold water, the salt, sugar, and corn syrup and whisk over high heat until the sugar has dissolved. Bring to a boil and cook, without stirring, until the mixture reaches 240ºF on a candy thermometer. Remove the sugar syrup from the heat and let cool to 210ºF.

Beat the gelatin mixture on low speed until smooth. Scrape down the sides and bottom of the bowl with a spatula. With the mixer running on low speed, slowly pour in the sugar syrup, avoiding the sides of the bowl, and beat until well combined, about 2 minutes. Gradually raise the mixer speed to medium-high and beat until the mixture is opaque and doubled in size, 12 to 17 minutes.

Grease a spatula with vegetable oil spray and, working quickly, transfer the marshmallow mixture to the prepared baking sheet. Run the spatula under water—this will make the next part easier—and use it to carefully smooth and spread the marshmallow mixture into the corners of the pan. Lift and lightly bang the pan on the counter to even out the marshmallow mixture, then dust the top with confectioners' sugar. Cover with plastic wrap and refrigerate for at least 4 hours or up to overnight to set.

Once set, run a knife around the edges of the baking sheet to loosen the marshmallow. Turn it out of the pan onto a cutting board.

Fill a small bowl with hot water. Dip a 2¾-inch (7mm) round cutter in the water and cut 12 marshmallows. Toss the marshmallow rounds in more confectioners' sugar, shaking off any excess, and set aside. (The marshmallows can be stored in an airtight container at room temperature for up to 2 weeks or in the refrigerator for up to 4 weeks.)

FOR THE GRAHAM CRACKERS: In a large bowl, whisk together the all-purpose flour, buckwheat flour, baking soda, and salt. Set aside.

In the bowl of a stand mixer fitted with the paddle attachment or in a medium bowl using a handheld mixer, cream the butter, granulated sugar, and brown sugar until light and fluffy on medium-high speed, 3 to 4 minutes.

Reduce the speed of the stand mixer to low and add a cup of the flour mixture followed by ¼ cup of the water. Allow to mix for a minute, scraping the sides of the bowl with a spatula as needed, then add the remaining flour and water and mix until combined.

Place the dough on a surface lightly dusted with flour and knead for a minute until smooth. Cut the dough in half and cover one half with plastic wrap. Place the other half of the dough between two pieces of parchment paper and roll to ¼-inch thickness. Refrigerate the rolled-out doughs for 15 minutes or until ready to bake. Repeat with the remaining half of the dough.

Meanwhile, preheat the oven to 350°F. Line two baking sheets with parchment paper. When ready to bake, remove one of the rolled-out doughs from the refrigerator and cut into circles using a 3-inch biscuit or round cookie cutter. Place the rounds on the prepared baking sheet about ½ inch apart from each other. Repeat with remaining half of the dough.

Bake for 10 minutes, then rotate the baking sheets and bake for about 10 minutes more, until the crackers are set and golden brown. Remove from the oven and allow to cool completely on the baking sheets. (The graham crackers can be stored in an airtight container at room temperature for up to a week.)

TO ASSEMBLE THE MARSHMALLOW PIES: Place a wire rack on a baking sheet. Arrange 12 graham crackers, bottom-side up, about 1 inch apart on the rack. Set aside the remaining 12 graham crackers.

In a small saucepan, bring 1 inch of water to a simmer over medium-low heat. Place half the chocolate in a small heatproof bowl and set it over the saucepan (be sure the bottom of the bowl does not touch the water). Melt the chocolate, stirring occasionally with a rubber spatula, until smooth, 2 to 3 minutes. Remove from the heat.

Dust off any excess confectioners' sugar from the marshmallows. Roll the sides of one marshmallow in the melted chocolate, keeping the top and bottom surfaces clean. Place the chocolate-dipped marshmallow on top of one graham cracker on the rack. Repeat with the remaining marshmallows.

One at a time, dip the tops of the reserved 12 graham crackers in the melted chocolate. Carefully shake off any excess. Top each chocolate-dipped marshmallow with a chocolate-dipped graham cracker. Refrigerate the marshmallow pies, still on the rack, until the chocolate is set, about 15 minutes.

Flip the marshmallow pies over so the undipped graham cracker is now facing up.

Place the remaining chocolate in the same small heatproof bowl and melt as above. Remove from the heat.

Dip the bottom of each marshmallow pie in the melted chocolate. Carefully shake off any excess. Return them to the rack and refrigerate until the chocolate is set, about 15 minutes. Serve. Store leftover pies in an airtight container or wrapped in plastic wrap at room temperature for up to 3 days.

PEANUT BUTTER SPICED WHOOPIE PIES

MAKES 8 TO 10

George Washington Carver created hundreds of uses for the humble peanut. Everything from flour, soap, and shaving cream to wood stains and skin lotion. That doesn't event count all the culinary possibilities. One I came up with was inspired by that great scientist, as well as a great chef, Nina Compton. Nina is from Saint Lucia in the Caribbean and owns Compère Lapin and Bywater American Bistro in New Orleans. She tops her chocolate coconut pecan cookies with curry salt. *If Nina Compton can curry cookies*, I thought, *and if George Washington Carver can come up with three hundred different ways to use peanuts, why can't I incorporate peanuts and curry into one of my favorite desserts, the whoopie pie?* I think it was a eureka moment, my own peanut-centric invention. You be the judge.

CAKES:

1¾ cups cake flour

1 cup packed light brown sugar

½ teaspoon kosher salt

1 teaspoon baking soda

2 large eggs

¾ cup plus 1 tablespoon whole milk

1 teaspoon vanilla extract

½ cup creamy peanut butter

¼ cup peanut oil

PEANUT BUTTER FILLING:

1 (8-ounce) package cream cheese, at room temperature

½ cup creamy peanut butter

3 tablespoons unsalted butter, at room temperature

1 cup confectioners' sugar

2 teaspoons garam masala

FOR THE CAKES: Preheat the oven to 325ºF. Line two baking sheets with parchment paper.

In a large bowl, whisk together the flour, brown sugar, salt, and baking soda. Set aside.

In the bowl of a stand mixer fitted with the whisk attachment or in a medium bowl using a handheld mixer, beat the eggs, milk, and vanilla on low speed until combined and smooth. Slowly add the flour mixture, beating until combined and smooth. If the batter is a little lumpy, add another tablespoon of milk. Add the peanut butter and oil and beat on medium speed for 4 to 5 minutes, until a smooth batter forms.

Scoop 2-tablespoon portions of the batter into rounds on the prepared baking sheets, spacing them 2 inches apart. Bake for 8 to 10 minutes, rotating the baking sheets halfway through, until the tops of the cakes spring back to the touch. Remove from the oven and allow to cool completely on the baking sheets.

FOR THE PEANUT BUTTER FILLING: Meanwhile, in the bowl of a stand mixer fitted with the paddle attachment or in a large bowl using a handheld mixer, beat the cream cheese on medium speed until smooth, about 2 minutes. Scrape down the sides of the bowl and add the peanut butter and butter. Beat on medium speed for about 1 minute, until incorporated.

Reduce the speed to low, add the confectioners' sugar and garam masala and beat until just incorporated, about 1 minute. Ramp up the speed to medium and beat for 1 minute. Scrape down the sides, getting all the way to the bottom of the bowl, then whip for another minute to make sure all the ingredients are well combined. Set aside until ready to use.

ASSEMBLE THE WHOOPIE PIES: Spread 2 tablespoons of the peanut butter filling over the flat side of one cooled cake. Place another cake on top, flat side down, to make a sandwich. Repeat to fill the remaining cakes. Wrap the whoopie pies in plastic wrap and refrigerate until ready to serve, for up to 3 days.

EVERYDAY JUNETEENTH

EVERYDAY JUNETEENTH

Every year we must remind successive generations that this event triggered a series of events that one by one defines the challenges and responsibilities of successive generations. That's why we need this holiday. —Al "Mr. Juneteenth" Edwards, Democratic Texas state representative who authored the legislation making Juneteenth a Texas state holiday in 1979

idden within the Juneteenth story are small moments of personal triumph that we will never know about. The entire society was transformed by emancipation, but how did it affect individual lives? Noisemaker-worthy celebrations are often followed by quieter victories.

My great-grandfather George Taylor left Oconee, Georgia—a town almost ten miles south of the University of Georgia, named after the Oconee branch of Creek Indians or Muskogean tribe—for a more prosperous future in Athens, and my great-aunts, two aunts, and uncle mostly stayed close. Then Hubert "Boley" Taylor, a Korean War veteran, married Mildred. They gave birth to my mother.

My mother, Janis Marie Taylor, graduated from high school in 1972 and voted for the first time in that year's presidential election (a victory her own mother never experienced). She made a living as a chicken factory worker. Forty-plus hours a week, dismembering chickens; rest was a luxury. In one day, I probably take as many coffee breaks and rejuvenation breaks as she got in a week. My midday lunches can take two hours or more sometimes. My mother showed me how to hustle; my experiences are teaching me it's fine to pause.

Even so, I'm unlearning the urge to plow through the day and rush on through to the next one. I pause. In the stillness, I connect with my whole self in ways my ancestors were not allowed. No space was held for them; their blue-collar jobs didn't include a lactation room, time off to vote, an atmosphere to speak openly about anxiety or hold a birthday lunch with cake and candles. I set my weekly intentions knowing that my responsibility is to remember to fill my heart with gratitude, to say my ancestors' names when the room is full and when nobody's listening.

This chapter's unfussy dishes are how I celebrate the quiet victories. Nothing says "celebration" like making waffles on a slow Saturday morning. Patting the salmon dry, cutting the okra, chopping the pecans—these things release weekday stress, for me, in an instant. Making a plate for family and friends and setting aside time for tidying my pantry—when I have made time to do these things, I count myself happy.

Even on the days that are not demarcated as holidays or holy days or special days, we should do special things for ourselves and the ones we hold dear. These small everyday traditions, these molecules of the ordinary, can have power and meaning, if we allow them to. Rituals of leisure and care are as much a testament to what Juneteenth has made possible as voting rights and desegregated buses are. It's these rituals that I want my son to embrace and feel and understand as important components of the legacy of Juneteenth.

COFFEE DAIQUIRI

MAKES 4 DRINKS

I have a massive coffee drawer that holds Nespresso pods, whole beans, a frother wand, a Turkish coffeepot—shall I keep going? At some point, I became obsessed with the ritual of coffee in the morning and afternoon (sometimes after dinner). No matter what, I sit down with my coffee. On weekends and holidays, I take more time to read the newspaper and even make espresso drinks beyond a cortado or latte. Here is my new favorite cocktail for every day. I typically make more coffee in the morning than I can drink; this is how I use up what's left. Brew your coffee using in your preferred method according to your taste.

Ice

1½ cups cold unsweetened brewed coffee

½ ounce Simple Syrup (note below)

1 ounce half-and-half

2 ounces dark rum

8 dashes of aromatic bitters

Ground cinnamon, for garnish

Fill a cocktail shaker with ice, add half the coffee, simple syrup, half-and-half, and rum and shake well to combine, until frothy. Strain into two cocktail glasses and top each with a dash of bitters and a sprinkle of cinnamon. Repeat with the remaining ingredients to make two more cocktails.

NOTE: To make simple syrup, combine 1¼ cup sugar to 1¼ cup water in a small saucepan. Bring to a boil over medium-high and cook until the sugar has dissolved, 4 to 5 minutes. Remove from the heat and let cool completely. Store in an airtight container in the refrigerator for several weeks.

FRUITS OF JUNETEENTH SMOOTHIE BOWL

SERVES 2 TO 4

My morning routine is pretty much the same; I try to get myself ready for the day first, before getting my son ready for his day. At one point, it was another way; I'd get up and tend to everyone except for myself, but after months of feeling depleted, I committed to centering myself first thing. On a perfect morning, I light lemongrass-scented incense and let the tunes on Alice Coltrane's *Journey in Satchidananda* album seep through my veins. Then I make a smoothie bowl (after coffee).

2 large purple sweet potatoes

2 cups whole milk

2 cups mixed summer berries, such as blueberries and strawberries, plus additional for garnish

½ mango, peeled, plus chopped mango for garnish

1 cup full-fat yogurt

2 teaspoons grated fresh ginger

¼ cup unsweetened coconut flakes, for garnish

Preheat the oven to 350°F. Roast the sweet potatoes until fork-tender, about 1 hour. Allow to cool completely, then scoop the flesh out of the skin and mash in a small bowl (you should have about 1 cup); discard the skin. (The sweet potatoes can be roasted ahead. Store in an airtight container in the refrigerator until ready to use, up to 3 days.)

In a blender or a food processor, combine the mashed sweet potatoes, milk, berries, mango, yogurt, and ginger and blend until smooth. Pour into a deep bowl and top with additional berries, mango, and the coconut flakes.

PECAN WAFFLES

MAKES 4 TO 6

Georgia, my home state, is the capital of pecan production in the United States. True to form, my hometown has plenty of pecan trees. In my growing-up days, we had a pecan tree in the backyard. Back before shelled pecans were more common in the store than whole pecans, I spent many an hour picking and shelling pecans. Waffles didn't become a signature of mine until I moved into an apartment in the East Point neighborhood of Atlanta as an adult. I was working at the American Cancer Society's national home office, but more memorable than that job was a midnight brunch I hosted, featuring waffles made with a cheap, fussy waffle maker. Fussy or not, it turned out good crispy waffles, made more delicious when drenched in butter. A dear friend, Tawonna Marshall, was dating a professional baseball player at the time, and he came through and joined us in playing Taboo, a popular 1990s board game. I hadn't yet perfected the pecan version of my waffle game back then. But now, years later, I've found that some pecans and a little cinnamon take these waffles up from very good to exceptional.

2 cups all-purpose flour

1½ teaspoons baking powder

¼ teaspoon ground cinnamon

¼ teaspoon fine sea salt

2 tablespoons packed dark brown sugar

3 large eggs

1 cup full-fat buttermilk, well shaken

4 tablespoons (½ stick) unsalted butter, melted, plus additional butter or peanut oil for greasing

⅓ cup pecans, coarsely chopped

Special equipment: waffle maker

Preheat the oven to 200ºF.

In a large bowl, whisk together the flour, baking powder, cinnamon, and salt until combined; set aside. In a medium bowl, whisk together the brown sugar, eggs, and buttermilk. Make a well in the dry mixture and pour the wet mixture into the center of the well. Whisk until everything is combined. Add the melted butter and pecans and stir again using a spatula until the batter is smooth.

Heat a waffle iron according to the manufacturer's instructions. Grease with additional butter and add the batter. Cook until golden brown, then transfer the waffle to a wire rack on a baking sheet and keep warm in the oven until ready to serve. Repeat with the remaining batter.

YELLOW SQUASH & CHEDDAR BISCUITS

MAKES 8

When I want a biscuit, I want a sturdy round one—and not from a fast-food spot. And yes, I'll devour two in one sitting; it's the reason biscuits are a special treat for me. (Though for many, biscuits are a frequent bread choice—whatever floats your boat.) For this vegetable-dotted version, I start with my go-to buttermilk biscuit recipe and take it in a direction inspired by the iconic squash-and-cheddar casserole. When making biscuits, it's all about quality flour, moisture, and even the outdoor temperature. On a morning when I decide to make more time for breakfast, I make this recipe, then fry up a sausage patty or cut a thin slice of tomato to stick between the biscuit.

2½ cups all-purpose flour, plus 2 teapoons for dusting

1 tablespoon baking powder

½ teaspoon baking soda

1 teaspoon kosher salt

1 teaspoon onion powder

2 teaspoons sugar

½ cup (1 stick) unsalted butter, cubed and chilled, plus additional for greasing

½ cup grated white cheddar cheese

¼ cup diced yellow squash (¼-inch dice)

1¼ to 1½ cups chilled full-fat buttermilk, well shaken

Special equipment: biscuit cutter

In a chilled large metal bowl, whisk together the flour, baking powder, baking soda, salt, onion powder, and sugar until combined. Add the butter and toss to coat in the flour mixture. Using your fingers or a pastry cutter, cut the butter into the flour mixture until lentil-size pieces form. Stir in the cheese and squash.

continued on page 250

Yellow Squash & Cheddar Biscuits, *continued*

Make a well in the center of the flour mixture and add the buttermilk, starting with 1¼ cups. Stir using a wooden spoon until the dough comes together.

Place the dough on a surface dusted with 2 teaspoons of flour and pat it gently into a ½-inch-thick rectangle. Fold the dough in thirds like a letter, then rotate it 90 degrees and pat it back out to a ½-inch-thick rectangle. Repeat two more times (a total of three rounds of folds), then pat the dough out to ¾-inch thickness.

Line a baking sheet with parchment paper. Dust a 3-inch biscuit cutter with flour and cut 8 biscuits from the dough (don't twist the cutter as you press down). Be gentle and avoid "warming" the biscuit dough with lots of touching. This technique ensures a beautiful rise. Gather the scraps and form as close to 3-inch biscuits as possible. Place on the prepared baking sheet and refrigerate for 15 minutes.

Preheat the oven to 425ºF.

Remove the biscuits from the refrigerator and bake until golden brown and puffed, 15 to 20 minutes. Allow to cool for 5 minutes before serving. Store leftover biscuits in an airtight container at room temperature for up to 2 days.

CARPE DIEM

For many Black Americans, everyday rituals and seasonal observances seem mundane. We take for granted the nightly hair scarf tying, rocking the pastel-colored suits for Easter photos, displaying the ceramic Black Santa at Christmastime, Sunday dinners at grandma's, and the homemade muscadine wine.

Take stock of the connective tissues or traditions that fortify us.

Talk to your family more about family reunions. Ask your mama: "Who in the family made the best potato salad?"

Seize the day

Find inspiration

Leon Bridges and Dawn Richard reverberated through my ears as I wrote my remembrances of Juneteenth parties. I revisited *Thoughts on Paper*, a coffee-table book with folk art by Alabama-born Thornton Dial. The museum exhibits of Emma Amos and Dawoud Bey brought pleasure.

Be a student

Get in the kitchen, cook. The end.

PRETZEL FRIED CHICKEN

SERVES 6

Many would call this dish chicken Milanese: the meat is pounded, then coated in seasoned bread crumbs. I suppose this chicken is inspired by Milanese, but it feels like an accessible, faster version of Sunday-dinner fried chicken. Use boneless, skinless chicken thighs (pounded), chicken breasts (butterflied and pounded), or chicken cutlets. I don't own a meat mallet, so I use my French rolling pin to obtain thin slices of chicken: just place the chicken on a cutting board, top with plastic wrap, and then pound away. Panko, a type of Japanese bread crumb, is a pantry staple for me and is the type of bread crumb many Milanese recipes call for. The finely crushed pretzels were an accident, as I needed more breading before making this quick weeknight dinner.

2 cups "everyday" olive oil

2 pounds boneless, skinless chicken cutlets

2 tablespoons fish sauce

1 cup all-purpose flour

½ teaspoon kosher salt, plus more as needed

½ teaspoon freshly ground black pepper

2 large eggs

2 tablespoons water

1 cup panko bread crumbs

10 pretzel sticks, finely ground in a food processor (1 cup)

4 teaspoons Chicken Salt (page 29)

In a large skillet, heat the olive oil over medium-high heat until shimmering. Place a wire rack on a baking sheet and set it next to the stove.

Season the chicken cutlets with the fish sauce and set aside.

Prepare a dredging station with three bowls or shallow baking dishes. Put the flour in the first bowl and season with salt and pepper. In the second bowl, whisk together the eggs and water. In the third, stir together the panko, ground pretzels, and chicken salt to combine.

Dredge each chicken piece in the flour first, shaking off any excess, then dip into the egg mixture, letting the excess drip off, and finally dredge in the bread crumb mixture to coat. Working in batches, add the chicken cutlets to the hot oil and shallow-fry for about 4 minutes per side, until the breading is golden brown and the cutlets reach 165ºF on an instant-read thermometer. Transfer to the wire rack and season with additional salt. Repeat with the remaining chicken. Serve hot.

BROILER SALMON

WITH ROMESCO

SERVES 8

Even though it was more than a month after Juneteenth, it felt celebratory to have friends visit us at the Maroon House in Athens, Georgia, so I hosted a dinner party. Lolis Eric Elie, a writer, filmmaker, and faculty member in UGA's low-residency narrative nonfiction MFA program, founded by the late writer and editor Valerie Boyd, brought his family, along with Bridgett Davis, a fellow Brooklynite and the author of *The World According to Fannie Davis*. I wanted to make something quick but special, and came up with this. The red pepper sauce, better known as romesco, was key.

1 (3- to 4-pound) skin-on side of salmon, bones removed

1 teaspoon fine sea salt

1 teaspoon freshly ground black pepper

1 cup Romesco (page 37)

1 tablespoon "everyday" olive oil

Position the top rack of the oven 6 inches from the broiler heat element and preheat the broiler to high. Line a baking sheet with foil.

Place the salmon skin-side down on the baking sheet. Pat dry with paper towels, then season with the salt and black pepper. Slather ½ cup of the romesco on top of the fish and drizzle with the olive oil.

Broil the salmon for 10 to 12 minutes, until browned. If it is browning too fast, bring it down to a lower rack. The internal temperature for silky, medium-doneness salmon is 125ºF; use an instant-read thermometer to check. Let the salmon rest for 3 to 4 minutes before serving with the remaining romesco.

GARLICKY OKRA & RICE

SERVES 4 TO 6

Gabrielle E. W. Carter is an Apex, North Carolina–based multimedia artist who uses art and farming and cooking as tools to talk about wealth, Black farmers, and food systems. Her curiosity about the politics of food catches. She is creating a homestead that will inspire a generation of young Black professionals to trade in their metropolitan careers for backyard gardening on their family properties. This recipe was inspired by something she did. In 2021, Carter dropped a line of T-shirts screen-printed with the words "Pay Black Farmers" and "Okra." She got next!

RICE:

2 cups long-grain white rice, preferably Carolina Gold

4 cups water

2 teaspoons kosher salt

1 bay leaf

OKRA:

1 pound okra, diced (about 3 cups)

4 tablespoons peanut oil

½ teaspoon kosher salt

¼ teaspoon red pepper flakes

2 teaspoons fish sauce

8 garlic cloves, finely chopped

⅛ cup peanuts, toasted and chopped

FOR THE RICE: Place the rice in a double strainer and rinse under cold running water until the water runs clear.

In a medium saucepan, combine the rice, water, salt, and bay leaf and then stir. Bring to a steady simmer over medium heat. Cover and cook for 15 to 20 minutes, without stirring. Remove the pan from the heat. Uncover the rice and let rest for at least 5 minutes. Fluff with a fork.

FOR THE OKRA: Using a slightly damp kitchen towel, wipe the okra to remove any debris. Chop into ½-inch pieces, discarding the woodsy top and point bottom.

Place a large skillet over medium-high heat and add the peanut oil. Add the okra, tossing well to coat, and sauté until it turns bright green, 2 to 3 minutes. Add the salt, red pepper flakes, and fish sauce and reduce the heat to medium. Then add in the chopped garlic. Cook for 7 to 8 minutes more, until the okra is caramelized to a deep brown.

Divide the rice evenly among individual serving bowls. Mound the okra on top, garnish with the peanuts, and serve. Store any leftovers in an airtight container in the refrigerator for 3 to 4 days.

SOUR CREAM & CHIVE CORNBREAD

SERVES 4

I can make classic Southern cornbread in my sleep. Over the years, I have played around with different fats—from bacon drippings to European butter to salted butter, buttermilk to Greek yogurt to sour cream. The flavor combination is both comforting and sophisticated. It reminds me of a baked potato, a bag of potato chips, and a fancy New Year's Eve appetizer.

2 cups yellow cornmeal

1 teaspoon kosher salt

1 teaspoon baking powder

2 teaspoons sugar

2 large eggs

2 tablespoons chopped fresh chives, plus chive blossoms with stems attached for top

1½ cups sour cream

8 tablespoons (1 stick) unsalted butter: 6 tablespoons melted, 2 tablespoons reserved for greasing

¼ teaspoon freshly ground black pepper

Preheat the oven to 425ºF and place a 10-inch cast-iron skillet in the oven to warm up.

In a large bowl, whisk together the cornmeal, salt, baking powder, and sugar. In a separate medium bowl, whisk together the eggs, chives, sour cream, the 6 tablespoons melted butter, and the pepper. Make a well in the dry ingredients and pour the wet ingredients into the well. Fold together using a rubber spatula until combined.

Carefully remove the hot skillet from the oven and add the remaining 2 tablespoons butter, swirling the hot skillet to melt the butter and coat. If needed, return the skillet to the oven and allow the butter to melt.

Once the butter is melted completely, pour the batter into the skillet (it will sizzle) and lay the chive blossoms with stems attached on top in a pattern. Return the skillet to the oven and bake for 25 to 30 minutes, until the cornbread is golden brown and a toothpick inserted in the center comes out clean. Allow to cool on a wire rack for 10 minutes and remove the whole chives before serving warm.

CHERRIES JUBILEE

SERVES 4

This effortless dessert brings the good vibes. Any dessert you set on fire is impressive. And its components remind me of my Black life—not a monolith. The origins of cherries jubilee go back to Queen Victoria's Golden Jubilee in the late 1800s, for which Auguste Escoffier, a famous French chef, prepared this dessert. If you are fortunate enough to shop in a place with an abundance of cherry varieties, do find Bing, sour, or Rainier cherries; they all work for this dessert. Hands down, they have the most distinctive and complex flavors.

4 scoops Honey Vanilla Ice Cream (page 185)

zest and juice of 2 tangerines (about 4 tablespoons zest and ½ cup juice)

4 tablespoons (½ stick) unsalted butter

½ cup sugar

¼ teaspoon kosher salt

1 tablespoon cornstarch

1 pound fresh Bing cherries, pitted

⅓ cup bourbon or American whiskey

Scoop the ice cream into individual bowls or one large serving bowl and freeze until ready to serve.

Zest and juice the tangerines; set the zest aside and pour the juice into a large saucepan. Add the butter and place the pot over medium heat. When the butter is melted, add the sugar, salt, and cornstarch and whisk until smooth. Add the cherries and stir to combine. Bring the mixture to a simmer, then cook 2 to 3 minutes, until the cherries have softened slightly and the sauce is thickened.

If cooking indoors, check for anything that could catch fire overhead or off to the sides of the stove. If cooking outdoors, make sure you have a place to put the hot pan. Pour the whiskey over the cherries and carefully ignite it with a long-nosed lighter or long match. Let the flame die out naturally.

Immediately pour the cherries and sauce into the bowls over the ice cream. Finish with the tangerine zest.

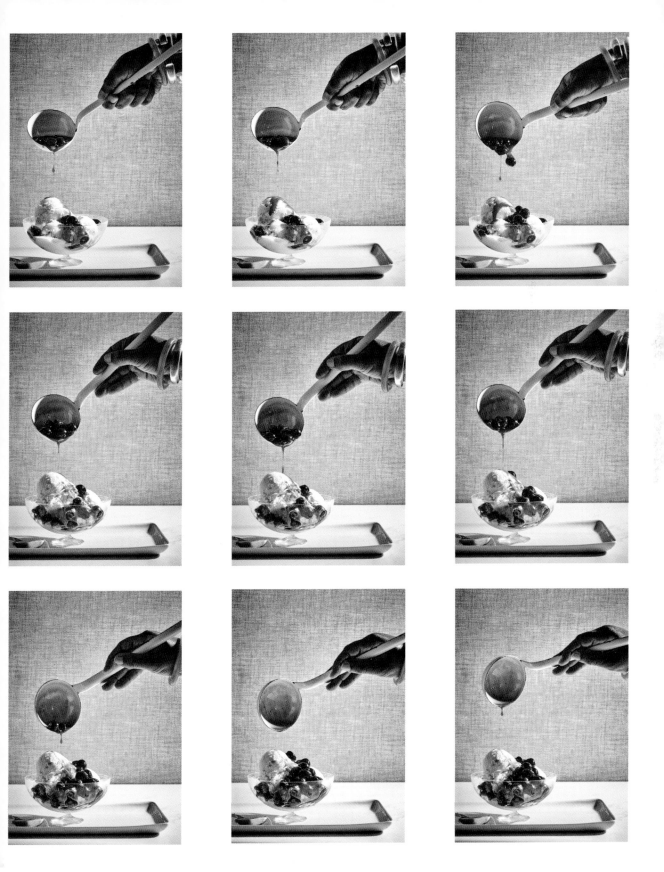

NOTES ON JUNETEENTH

I'll call this a poor man's bibliography. I'm not a historian; I'm a curious person who reads a lot and spends equally as much time in the kitchen. Throughout the text, I name-drop books, songs, people, and places that can lead one down a rabbit hole—bread crumbs. Many readers will pick up on the cultural cues in the headnotes and essays; they are intentional. The following is from my notes, a list of things that helped shape this cookbook.

Books

Anne Byrn, *American Cookie: The Snaps, Drops, Jumbles, Tea Cakes, Bars & Brownies That We Have Loved for Generations* (New York: Rodale Books, 2018).

Harriet Cole, *How to Be: A Guide to Contemporary Living for African Americans* (New York: Simon & Schuster, 2000).

Tommie D. Boudreau and Alice M. Gatson, *African Americans of Galveston (Images of America)* (Mount Pleasant, SC: Arcadia Publishing, 2013).

Articles

Deborah Douglas, " 'I Wish Juneteenth Could Remain Underground, Secret, and Sacred,' " *Vice*, June 22, 2021, https://www.vice.com/en/article/akg7qp/juneteenth-federal-holiday-2021-history.

"An historical look at Milwaukee's Juneteenth Day 1979– to present," June 20, 2019, *Milwaukee Journal-Sentinel*, https://www.jsonline.com/picture-gallery/news/local/2019/06/18/historical-look-milwaukees-juneteenth-day-celebrations/1489095001/.

Aaron Hutcherson, "The Seasoning that Inspires Salty Looks and Kanye Hooks," *Taste*, August 16, 2018, https://tastecooking.com/seasoning-inspires-salty-looks-kanye-hooks/.

Casey Gerald, "The Art of the Black Escape," *New York*, August 8, 2019, https://nymag.com/intelligencer/2019/08/the-black-art-of-escape.html.

Rosiland Cummings-Yeates, "Watermelon and the seeds of Black freedom," *The Takeout*, July 2, 2021, https://thetakeout.com/watermelon-and-the-seeds-of-black-freedom-1847207443.

Cynthia Greenlee, "On eating watermelon in front of white people: 'I'm not as free as I thought,' " *Vox*, August 29, 2019, https://www.vox.com/first-person/2019/8/29/20836933/watermelon-racist-history-black-people.

Daniel Vaughn, "Recipe: Smoked Turkey Legs," *Texas Monthly*, September 25, 2020, https://www.texasmonthly.com/bbq/recipe-smoked-turkey-legs/.

Kayla Stewart, "Turkey Leg Hut has become a bastion of Houston's Black culture—and a gentrification lightning rod," *Washington Post*, May 14, 2021, https://www.washingtonpost.com /food/2021/05/14/turkey-leg-hut -houston/.

Mandy Leonard, "Fannin County uncovers first records of Negro State Fair, held 1911 in Bonham," *North Texas E-News*, August 25, 2021, http://www .ntxe-news.com/artman/publish /article_125779.shtml.

Therese Nelson, "Hot Sauce in my Veins," *Taste*, May 16, 2018, https:// tastecooking.com/hot-sauce-veins/.

Adrian Miller, "The media has erased the long history of Black barbeque, skewing our understanding," *Washington Post*, August 13, 2021, https://www .washingtonpost.com/outlook /2021/08/13/media-has-erased -long-history-black-barbecue -skewing-our-understanding/.

Public Collections and Exhibits

"Marion Butts: Lens on Dallas," Collection of the Dallas Public Library, https:// dallaslibrary2.org/marionbutts/.

Kathryn Siefker, Associate Curator of Exhibit Content, "NAACP YOUTH COUNCIL PICKET LINE, 1955 TEXAS STATE FAIR: 'Don't Sell Your Pride for a Segregated Ride,' " Bullock Museum "Artifact Spotlight," https://www.the storyoftexas.com/discover/artifacts /naacp-state-fair-spotlight-012315.

Rhonda Evans, Assistant Chief Librarian, JBH Research and Reference Division, Schomburg Center for Research in Black Culture, "Researching Juneteenth Celebrations at The New York Public Library," New York Public Library blog, June 19, 2017, https://www.nypl.org /blog/2017/06/19/celebrating-juneteenth.

Peter Simek, "The Long, Troubled, and Often Bizarre History of the State Fair of Texas," *D Magazine*, September 26, 2019, https://www.dmagazine.com/front burner/2019/09/the-long-troubled -and-often-bizarre-history-of-the -state-fair-of-texas/.

Film/Video

Solange Knowles, director. *When I Get Home*. Released by Apple Music, available on all platforms, 2019.

Los Angeles Times Food, "L.A. Times Food Bowl's Food Forum: Red Drinks for Juneteenth," YouTube video, streamed live June 15, 2021, https://www.youtube .com/watch?v=mu65MXVAKRc.

WNYC, "Why Juneteenth Continues to Matter," YouTube video uploaded June 20, 2018, https://www.youtube.com /watch?v=feSreeZzxWw.

Websites

www.juneteenth.com

thedrinkingcoach.com (official website of Tiffanie Barriere, Mixologist and Creative)

INDEX

Praise for *Watermelon & Red Birds*

"*Watermelon & Red Birds* is a call for us all to celebrate Black joy and freedom in its many facets. Nicole Taylor has gifted the world with a breathtaking cookbook that is grounded in history and tradition while keeping one eye on the ever-evolving nature of culture, customs, and foodways. This book reminds us that Black folks should own and drive the way we celebrate our historical milestones, and what better way to do so than over a full plate with family and friends."

Bryant Terry,

James Beard Award–winning author of *Black Food* and editor in chief of 4 Color Books

• • •

"Juneteenth is a newly minted holiday but an old celebration. In *Watermelon & Red Birds*, Nicole Taylor provides an impressive array of new recipes for a new generation to tip a glass of red drink and savor the flavors of this new jubilee. Each step of the way, she reminds us of the history and evolution of this most delectable and needful American holiday."

Lolis Eric Elie,

coauthor of *Rodney Scott's World of BBQ*

"As with every Nicole Taylor gathering I've attended, *Watermelon & Red Birds* is vivid with joy and aliveness. The story of Juneteenth that grounds this festive recipe collection celebrates the places we've been and the people we've become. This cookbook, rich with poignant history, refreshing anecdotes, and Taylor's singular ability to convey the global reach of southern-inspired cuisine, is the spirited guide many of us have been craving. Consider this timely treasure a labor of love for Black American food culture, and an invitation to embrace its evolving ingenuity and creativity all year long."

Osayi Endolyn,

James Beard–Award winning food and culture writer

• • •

"The prolific Nicole Taylor has taken us on a brilliant exploration of African American culture in delicious bites. *Watermelon & Red Birds* is full of amazing stories but most of all it stays true to the culture. This is a must-read for all."

JJ Johnson,

chef and founder of FIELDTRIP